MW01598161

The People's U.S. Constitution: Academics & Law Professors Can Go Elsewhere

By Jeff Brown, Your Humble Civil Servant

© 2016 Lulu Author. All rights reserved.
ISBN 978-1-312-25182-3

jeffbrowncareercoaching.com

The People's U.S. Constitution: Academics and Law Professors Go Elsewhere, Copyright © 2016 by Inner Projection™, Inc.

Written by Jeff Brown

All rights reserved.

No part of this book may be used or duplicated without the written permission of the copyright holder.

For information about how to order large quantities of this e-book, contact: Inner Projection™, Inc. 8601 International Ave. Suite 275 Canoga Park, CA 91304

E-Mail: professorjeffreypbrown@gmail.com
URL: jeffbrowncareercoaching.com

Why I've Written This, What You're Getting, and What You're Not Getting

OK, I am going tell you right off the bat why I wrote this book. A basic understanding of the U.S. Constitution is as essential for ALL Americans as it is for us to play the latest video game. OK, of course I'm joking, who wants to play video games? There are obviously way more people reading books than playing video games. But let's just say this isn't true and that people prefer video games to reading, as absurd as that sounds. I ask you now to stop playing Call of Duty, The Walking Dead: The Game – Season 2, Game of Thrones, Wolfenstein: The New Order just long enough to get through this information that only applies to everything of a critical nature that goes on in this country. It will do a body, mind, and spirit good. Believe me. Then you can get back to killing the undead and soldiering like a boss.

But why is it that games are so popular while the Constitution goes virtually ignored? (And I'm also talking about all those people on the Internet who say they support the Constitution while having never read it. I never imagined so many members of Congress were online). Well, outside the obvious—video games are a heck of a lot more fun than reading, anything!—most people may want to know about the U.S. Constitution, but it certainly is a bear to read. I mean, have you ever sat down to read it? Let me tell you right now that without some form of layperson's interpretation there is going to be little to no understanding with all that arcane, passé, generic stuff going on.

Why?

Well . . . it's law, silly! Have you ever read any law code? (OK, it's more general than law code, but it is law. You get the point) Here's an example. Try to stay awake while reading. But don't fret, a living, breathing human is just on the other side. I will be right back with my scintillating commentary. Here is a little light reading from Title 18: Part II, Chapter 208, § 3161, section (d) (1). Enjoy.

(1) If any indictment or information is dismissed upon motion of the defendant, or any charge contained in a complaint filed against an individual is dismissed or otherwise dropped, and thereafter a complaint is filed against such defendant or individual charging him with the same offense or an offense based on the same conduct or arising from the same criminal episode, or an information or indictment is filed charging such defendant with the same offense or an offense based on the same conduct or arising from the same criminal episode, the provisions of subsections (b) and (c) of this section shall be applicable with respect to such subsequent complaint, indictment, or information, as the case may be . .

COMA!!!!!

Really! Who goes to college to actually, and truthfully mind you, use a God-given, human brain to not only understand this stuff but also somewhere along the line became convinced that they did the right thing by going to college to ingest this stuff on a regular basis? Look me in the eye lawyer person and tell me the truth.

Ah, ha! I knew you couldn't!

I digress.

Regardless of the number of people lying to themselves in saying that they became a lawyer simply to come to the aid or their fellow humans, this law stuff is downright nasty. More specifically, some of the most boring stuff this side of your high school history teacher. I have several lawyer friends who told me that the last thing they wanted to do in life was paperwork. Guess what? That's about all lawyers do is read, read, read this stuff. I know! Right!

But don't worry, I am here to the rescue.

And what's good about me is that I'm just some average non-lawyer, non-politician, non-whatever who doesn't care about protecting his image and will talk down law and its being boring, or convoluted, or mistreated by those in power in government at the federal and state level. Actually, I have read those books that explain the seven articles and twenty-seven amendments of the Constitution, and many never give you the layperson lowdown of the nasty or under-belly of law, government, and its adherents.

No problem here. By telling you a lot of truths and not holding back on some of the foolishness of humankind in regards to law, the Constitution, and our illustrious government, I am not going to lose tenure, my job, or my seat in the Senate. So there! you Constitutional commentaryers.

In addition, I am not going into a lot of boring detail or history of the Constitution, like a lot of those Constitutional authors do, because I am lucky if I can get just a few people to understand the basics using everyday non-legalese language and minimal historical minutia. If you want extensive history about stuff that is moot or no longer applies to us Americans today, you will have to go to one of those books written by a Harvard law professor or historian with endless credits and half the alphabet after her name.

That's not going to happen here. Sorry.

As an American who has little time to spend on things outside of work, family, a little leisure and play, I just want the basics. For it certainly is important to know the basics, so that when making political decisions, when voting for a political figures, we all have a little better idea of what is out there regarding our God-given or Constitutional rights. And don't forget knowing who's in power and the role you—the average citizen— plays, as limited as it may be at this point. Another good reason to read this book, and those similar to it, is to help guide our country back into the hands of the people. You want to know why more and more are falling into the lower class, and why fewer and fewer possess more and more of U.S. wealth? This book is a good start. We do not want to go back to monarchs and despots, for sure. Equally important is keeping our politicians on the up and up with our basic understanding of Constitutional rights and obligations. For we certainly do have them.

However, just to let you see why this stuff is important, consider the mere fact that you as an individual do not have a Constitutional right to vote. That is right. Moreover, that your right to privacy is protected only so far. In addition, that a great number of Constitutional rights are at the federal level only, not at the state level, meaning, that many of your Constitutional rights are null and void by state constitutions. A lot of time the Constitution says "Here's your rights, but only if We (federal) are involved." State? What say ye?

OK, now you know why I have written this book. My approach. Why you should read it. And what you need to do right now. That's right. Read!

Go to it. I will see you inside.

The US Constitution: Introductory Summary

The US Constitution is the supreme law of the land. It provides the framework—key word here—for the organizing of the US Government. It does not lay down laws in specifics, but was left open ended enough for interpretation and, ultimately, changes or amendments. For there are many things that the founding fathers could not and did not foresee that would require changes or changes to the original text.

But the Constitution was and is not found to be perfect. Justice Thurgood Marshal stated that the US Constitution was "defective from the start, requiring several amendments, a civil war, and momentous social transformation to attain the system of constitutional government, and its respect for the individual freedoms and human rights, we hold as fundamental today." Well, that's debatable too, but you get the point.

And even though it still has not been perfected, it is reaching toward perfection, and even from the outset with great chance for perfection coming from imperfect composers, a minor miracle occurred: "When you assemble a number of men to have the advantage of their joint wisdom, you inevitably assemble with those men all their prejudices, their passions, their errors of opinion, their local interests, and their selfish views. From such an assembly can a perfect production be expected? It therefore astonishes me, Sir, to find this system approaching so near to perfection it does" (Benjamin Franklin).

Perfection is not something that comes easy, nor should it be in regarding the legal ramifications of a document that protects the rights and freedoms of hundreds of millions of citizens. One can observe the strength of the document and the will of the people to maintain its integrity in the sheer volume of rejected amendments. Over the years, there have been hundreds and hundreds of proposed amendments. For example, from the 101st to 106th sessions of Congress over 800 amendments were proposed. As any captain knows, maintaining the integrity of the hull of his craft is primary in keeping the ship afloat. So far, the craft has yet to reach perfection, but the hull's integrity is on the up 'n up.

However, what specifically does the US Constitution entail? What is it all about above and beyond getting too lost in the details and sometimes moot points or arcane language? We will get into this as we go through the seven articles, their sections, and the twenty-seven amendments, but for now, let us take a general overview of the Constitution.

The US Constitution defines the three main branches of the government: the legislative branch consisting of Congress; the executive, with the president at the head; and the judicial or Supreme Court. These branches are said to provide checks and balances and a "separation of power"' or those powers given; however, others believe that this power is not so separate that there is an overlapping of powers: "The constitutional convention of 1787 is supposed to have created a government of separated powers. It did nothing of the sort. Rather, it created a government of separated institutions sharing powers" (political scientists Richard Neustadt).

More than anything, however, can be found the importance of the human element above and beyond any words one may find on paper: "I often wonder whether we do not rest our hopes too much upon constitutions, upon laws, and upon courts. These are false hopes; believe me, these are false hopes. Liberty lies in the heart of men and women; when it dies there, no constitution, no laws, no court can save it" (Judge Learned Hand). One can see the limitations of this document if the minds and hearts of a majority of the men and women who use it become corrupt in the extreme.

The Constitution has inherent "checks and balances" beyond what many may understand: "You must first enable the government to control the governed; and in the next place oblige it to control itself" (James Madison). This document is meant to be a guideline, but it is up to the majority of those superior in insight, moral and ethical appeal to do what is best to protect and serve all; but even more importantly, those in the minority whose inalienable rights may be infringed upon must be looked after, for if the few cannot be served then the many have no right being borne up by Constitutional law. But it is the human element in the equation that is the most interesting, important, and often times, humbling.

"Reader, suppose you were an idiot. And suppose you were a member of Congress. But I repeat myself" (Mark Twain).

And our humanity shines imperfect in the very statement that set the stage for aiding us in reaching toward mass-character perfection: "We hold these truths to be self-evident: That all men are created equal; that they are endowed by their Creator with certain unalienable rights; that among these are life, liberty, and the pursuit of happiness..."

This written by a man who owned slaves and said document signed by many in the same situation. This written by a man full of contradiction, a man like you and I, imperfect yet working toward betterment, working with a vision of perfection in mind—that which motivates but can never be obtained by mere mortals. Who else but a man of contradiction would say of Thomas Paine's simple prose in Common Sense: "No writer has exceeded Paine in ease and familiarity of style: in perspicuity of expression, happiness of elucidation, and in simple, unassuming language." –Thomas Jefferson

But who can raise his or her hand and not claim contradiction, that which is so difficult to see by its possessor yet seen plain as day by friends and even acquaintances. As humans, this is our inheritance, but it is something that we have worked to amend from the start of these United States:

Many found themselves deselected: the slaves of Massachusetts petitioning for their "unalienable rights to freedom" in 1777; white men without property seeking the vote; The Cherokee Nation believing that American Indians should be protected under the Constitution; women arguing that they too were a part of "We the People." As stated above, the biggest human contradiction came from the founding penman himself, Thomas Jefferson, a slave owner, owner of men not free physically or politically. Nevertheless, it is the document that began it all and has—as its composers and ancestors—matured over time, working toward an inherent ideal through the imperfect natures of the men and woman who mold and shape this work of political and ethical art. Please follow along as we take a compulsory look at this most liberating of documents known to humankind.

The People's US Constitution: Article I, The Legislative Branch

Since those taking political office and serving in the armed forces must pledge to support the Constitution, and every citizen informally / indirectly pledges to do so—naturalized citizens directly--why this isn't taught every year in high school is beyond comprehension. The people who take office and pledge to serve this country are those that we vote for, ergo we must know the Constitution well enough to know what those we put in office are pledging to. This is the main reason behind why I've taken on this task of "spreading the word." And I'm not talking about a few School House Rock political-education videos (look them up on Youtube if you're a youngin').

Keep in mind that this document was written a long time ago when there were a lot fewer people, more open prejudice, and ideas that have since run their course. As I cover the articles of the Constitution, I will not cover all the points that have fallen by the wayside (i.e.: The three fifths compromise, found in Article 1, Section 2, Paragraph 3, states that slaves were regarded 3/5th of a person for tax purposes). These exceptions will be taken up in the twenty-seven amendments covered later. I will touch upon a few but the Amendments will be handled specifically and one at a time.

I will also not be going into minor points that can merely be looked up in the thousands of books and articles on the Internet. My purpose here is to expose as briefly as possible the essentials of the Constitution to those who are unschooled in the essentials. I do not write to merely duplicate the detail that already exists that which is ignored by the majority because of the work involved in deciphering its complexity. I hope that along the way I can provide some interesting if not thought provoking points that will connect to the majority.

But at the same time, I will attempt to keep the reader awake and engaged with pertinent and hopefully interesting points as well as using a little bit of the old tongue-in-cheek to point to the general human foibles inherent in any work of man or woman, its inconsistencies, and, let's just get right down to it, the downright boredom of law. Some may find law constantly fascinating and enthralling but those couple dozen people already work in law. For those of us who find it dry, drab, boring . . . hmmmmmm, let's see, anything else? Yeah, just drop-dead, fall fast-asleep, IBM-technical manual un-stimulating . . . well, I am here to help.

In addition, at times when sections become lengthy, I will include the specific Constitutional text merely as a point of reference. The first few articles are relatively brief. Some articles, especially 8, 9, and 10, will include more of the specific text because of their length. It would be difficult to follow along without the actual Constitutional text.

Let's get into it.

The Constitution consists of a preamble, seven articles, twenty-seven amendments, and a paragraph certifying its enactment by the constitutional convention. I will begin with the meat of the document, or those sections that set the guidelines for our US Democracy, the articles.

Article One lays out the legislative powers of the bicameral Congress (the lower house, House of Representatives, and the upper house, the Senate) or the "purse strings" of our government that is responsible for creating and modifying tax laws and levying taxes.

This is the longest article of the seven, most likely because **The Constitution** replaced **The Articles of Confederation and Perpetual Union** in which the framework for Congress—the legislative—had already been laid out to a great extent. Before the US Constitution was written, there was no Executive or Judicial. Interestingly, Articles II and III, those explaining the Executive and Judicial are briefer and less rigid.

Article One lays out the federal powers of Congress, among them the right to collect taxes, borrow money, regulate commerce, establish post offices, and declare war.

Section 1: The Legislature

There are certain powers vested in Congress, but because of the separation of powers, Congress cannot delegate legislative authority to other branches. However, Congress has been given the power by the Supreme Court to delegate regulatory powers to executive agencies. It also has the power to investigate and compel cooperation with investigation, and even though the Constitution does not specifically mention this power, the Supreme Court has once again affirmed these powers.

Herein one can see the interpretive and malleable "framework" nature of the Constitution. And even though the Supreme Court has broadly interpreted the investigative powers of Congress, the rights of those called before a congressional investigation (whether it be as an alleged communist or professional athlete who consumes performance enhancing drugs) are protected by the **Bill of Rights**, the first ten amendments to the Constitution. Again, your checks and balances.

Section 2: The House

The House of Representatives is the "People's House." To reside in the People's House, you need to be at least 25 years-old and to have been a US citizen for seven years, and when you get elected, you will reside in that state from which elected. Moreover, you are elected "by the People of the several States," that would now be fifty, not the original 13 (can you name them?), every two years.

So you may be saying that is a quick revolving door. And that's the point, for you supporters of short terms. This way the members stay close to the people; this way there is difficulty in building relationships that would empower them and lead to corruption or greater corruption. Not that all who become empowered are corruptible or corrupt, but there are always a number who go that route. So this is a very important point for those who support term limits. However, some complain that in constantly running for office that is what politicians will have to do, focus on running for office and not long-term goals. It's a basic you-can't-have-your-cake-and-eat-it melodrama.

This section also lays out how taxes are to be "apportioned among the several states," and in order to do this, the population of the US is to be counted every 10 years.

Initially, this section of the Constitution said that the number of representatives should not be greater than one for every 30,000 citizens. Today, that would be a lot of representatives, so Congress has set the number to a limit of 435.

This section also explains how the governors of a state that lose a representative can call a special election, and how the House of Representatives shall chose the Speaker of the House and other officers and shall have the sole power of impeachment.

Section 3: The Senate

This section sets out the number of senators for each state as two, to be chosen by the legislature of a given state and that the term shall be for six years.

This section also explains how the terms of office for senators are rotated in three groups so that the entire Senate is not up for election at the same time. It also explains that if a vacancy occurs during recess, the governor of said state may temporarily appoint a new senator until the next election.

We also discover where the VP of the United States will be spending most of his time. He is upped to president, President of the Senate, for the duration of his term in office. But don't get excited. According to John Adams, being President of the Senate meant little more than a glorified title of one who sat all day long trying to stay awake while men (and now women) droned on and on.

Here we find that the Senate will choose its own officers and president pro tempore or one who will stand in when the VP is absent. Once again, don't get excited. This is more a ceremonial office, like the Queen of England, than one of power. The power of the Senate actually resides in the majority leader.

Here is a general laundry list of the remaining points of Section 3:

The Senate shall have the sole Power to try all impeachments. When sitting for that Purpose, they shall be on Oath or Affirmation. When the President of the United States is tried, the Chief Justice shall preside: And no Person shall be convicted without the Concurrence of two thirds of the Members present.

Judgment in Cases of Impeachment shall not extend further than removal from Office, and disqualification to hold and enjoy any Office of honor, Trust or Profit under the United States: but the Party convicted shall nevertheless be liable and subject to Indictment, Trial, Judgment and Punishment, according to Law.

Section 4: Elections, Meetings

This one is pretty straight forward. Congress sets for itself the time, place, and manor of holding elections for Senators and Representatives. (Remember, lawyers put this document together, and, as I have said before, this is not law code but a Constitution painted with broad brush strokes to enable amendment). However, Section 4 then says, "Just kidding." Well, mostly, for Congress can then change time and manor but not place. However, states provide the basic qualifications for voting in federal elections, but Congress may determine the procedures under which votes are cast.

Pretty basic housekeeping, not something you will use in making your next voting decision; however, it may come in handy if you're playing Congress some time with your siblings and you want to play Election and Assembly; you'll be in the driver's seat.

Oh, one thing more. Congress tells itself that it should assemble once a year, every year and that meeting will be on the first Monday in December. But how long is a session? Well, it depends which bicameral part of Congress you are talking about.

Over a 30 year period, from 1969 to 1999, over sixteen sessions (91st to 106th), the House averaged 287 days (longest session 350 days; shortest 137 days) while the Senate averaged 308 days over the same period (longest session 384 days; shortest 162 days); therefore, showing us that the Senate works harder than the House, and once again proving that the common man is lazier than the erudite elitist who works hard to make things happen with their bigger brains.

OK, just kidding. Doesn't tell us much, does it?

On with the sections.

Section 5: Membership, Rules, Journals, Adjournment

Each House shall be the judge of the elections, returns and qualifications of its own members, and a majority of each shall constitute a quorum to do business; but a smaller number may adjourn from day to day, and may be authorized to compel the attendance of absent members, in such manner, and under such penalties as each House may provide.

Each House may determine the rules of its proceedings, punish its members for disorderly behavior, and, with the concurrence of two thirds, expel a member.

At one time, due to the occasional offense, Congress refused to seat elected legislators even though they met the qualifications set out by the Constitution. Certainly, historically an offense occurred here and there, so what is a Court to do? The Court determined that even if a majority voted out a member of the House or Senate, a dismissal would not occur unless the offense had taken place during that member's term.

The lesson for the kids?

Simple. If you find your classmate's baseball cards will just not come out of your backpack, or you "borrow" someone's jacket without asking but just can't seem to give it back (even though your mom's been screaming at you to do so for over a week), just make sure these alleged offenses occur before the school term officially begins (summer and winter break are ideal). If you can just hold off that offense until a school break comes, your guilt is absolved.

Kids?

(A loud cacophony of adolescents)

"Thanks Congress!"

OK, Congress is made up of people, and yes, mostly men. Sorry ladies, I know you are catching up with the men in many ways, but I pray you do not in this case: "disorderly behavior." Back in the day, there was a very famous duel, which you are aware of, yes? Hamilton vs. Burr.

Hamilton said some negative things about Burr's character—or as Burr would have said, "slanders"—over a period of time, so Burr called him out. Hamilton accepted, and the rest is history. (If you do not know that history, you can get a brief version of it on the Got Milk? commercial. I'm sure YouTube has it.)

So you say, of course, "Back in the day when men were less civilized, I can understand why Congress would need this passage in the Constitution, but today? No." OK, so you think Congress has not gotten physical in recent years. Think again.

In 2004, Rep. Cunningham was mistreating a congressional staffer Rep. Jim Moran who ended up shoving Cunningham into a congressional cloakroom. Then there is the more recent incident of Senator McCain allegedly engaging in fisticuffs with an Arizona Congressman. So what is a poor Congress to do with these testosterone enhanced politicians? Well, you may or may not be privy to that information. It is up to Congress, unless it happens to be caught on CSPAN that is.

Each House shall keep a journal of its proceedings, and from time to time publish the same, excepting such parts as may in their judgment require secrecy; and the yeas and nays of the members of either House on any question shall, at the desire of one fifth of those present, be entered on the journal.

So you want to know what is going on in Congress. Many do, but then again, there is that part of the passage that says, "Accepting such parts as may in their judgment require secrecy." We can only hope good judgment is used here, yes?

Neither House, during the session of Congress, shall, without the consent of the other, adjourn for more than three days, nor to any other place than that in which the two Houses shall be sitting.

In January of 2012, President Obama claimed to use Section 5, Article 1 to make an appointment to the Director of Consumer Finance Protection Bureau as well as three people to the National Labor Relations Board. Yet many complained that Congress was in session, so this simply ignores the Constitution, which is an issue, of course.

According to experts, the executive and legislative branch have over-extended themselves in the appointment process. And to question an appointment or appointments often involves extensive court hearings. So a lot of how the Constitution is interpreted is up for debate. On occasion, the Court has to get involved to determine how the Constitution should be interpreted, but how it is interpreted depends on who the nine judges are. In addition, they only have so much time and can't get to all that is requested of them. These are a few points most don't consider when talking about how the Constitution is interpreted.

Section 6: Compensation

The Senators and Representatives shall receive a Compensation for their Services, to be ascertained by Law, and paid out of the Treasury of the United States.

We have to pay these guys too? Certainly, but can you believe that Congress at one time could vote itself a pay raise without review. Nice!

Just imagine you doing this at work. "Ah, Mr. Jensen, I'll be getting a 10% . . . No, wait a minute . . ." Thinking to self, let's see, bicoastal homes, new Mercedes when it gets dirty, ah . . . "Jensen, make that a 50% increase." Mr. Jensen, your boss, now replaces you with a new guy.

Finally, in 1992 the 27th Amendment was passed which said that Congress could vote itself a pay raise, but it would not take effect until after the next election of representatives. Ahhhhhh, you say. That will limit interest, sure enough. Because who wants to vote a pay hike if some other guy's gonna get it? But then again that's why they get their buddies to surround them in the Senate. Capisce?

They shall in all Cases, except Treason, Felony and Breach of the Peace, be privileged from Arrest during their Attendance at the Session of their respective Houses, and in going to and returning

from the same; and for any Speech or Debate in either House, they shall not be questioned in any other Place.

This states that when Congress is in session, they are privileged from civil arrest, except for misdemeanors (threats, theft, indecent exposure, traffic violations) and felonies (murder, rape, arson, sale of illegal drugs, grand theft, kidnapping). For misdemeanors, one is incarcerated for twelve months or less; for felonies, twelve months or more. This all means that Congress can be arrested for . . . well, a lot. They can get away with parking tickets and such but not much worse. (I know; I worked at Logan Airport in Boston in the ticket division, and VIP's always get their tickets dismissed.)

But remember, we are dealing with lawyers here and loop holes. The point being that if an elected official in one house or the other gets arrested, while in jail there is obvious limitation as to legislative power. Remember, these people are in charge of creating laws and a lot of important stuff. So if in prison, for example, can a Congressperson vote? Maybe. To be sure, run this experiment: get a senator or representative arrested during a session and see what happens. There have been congressional representatives arrested for DWI and money laundering, but those are felonies, so I don't know of any who have got off because of Section 6. Call me if you find out. (But I'm guessing that since these are members of Congress, there's more that they can get away with than you think. They are kind of sneaky and slippery that way, ya know.)

In addition, those in Congress cannot be sued during congressional debate for slander.

With all these "exceptions," you can understand why these VIPs can get a big head.

No Senator or Representative shall, during the Time for which he was elected, be appointed to any civil Office under the Authority of the United States which shall have been created, or the Emoluments whereof shall have been increased during such time; and no Person holding any Office under the United States, shall be a Member of either House during his Continuance in Office.

What's that you say?

This is known as the **ineligibility clause** which prevents Congress from gaining too much power and money. Just imagine if members of Congress could go around creating jobs and setting salaries for themselves so that later they could take those same jobs and / or salaries for themselves. If that were the case, then it wouldn't be called Congress. It would be called Enron. Also this disallowed the executive or judicial from working in Congress at the same time to encourage separation of powers. But as you know, this hasn't stopped Congress from gaining lots of funding or fattening of their wallets via other means.

Section 7: Revenue Bills, Legislative Process, Presidential Veto

All bills for raising Revenue shall originate in the House of Representatives; but the Senate may propose or concur with Amendments as on other Bills.

Basically, revenue bills begin in the House. The point being that *we the people* would like to keep tabs on how Congress goes about raising money, meaning, the House is closer to the people so the bills begin here.

Don't believe me? OK (if not, just pretend you're in disbelief here. Humor me for the sake of a point). In the House there's not as much prestige as the Senate. Heck, the job only lasts for two years. You've got six years in the Senate. That's a lot of days off (remember Section 4? The Senate averages some 50 days off a year. Nice work if you can get it).

Think about it. If you were looking to impress someone, would you like to say you are a Representative or a Senator? Ah, see? Have you ever seen a movie where the prestigious politician is a Representative? It's not Rep. John McLaughlin, Rep. Robert Kelley, Rep. Bail Organ. NO! They're all Senators. You get the picture.

But I'd like to pause a moment and really get to the meat of the issue here. It's nice to vote these people into office and to know a bit about the Constitution, but do you *ever* watch CSPAN to see what is going on regarding our money? The raising of it or the taxing of it? I thought so. Why? Because most people are busy, and once the person is in office, we go back to our jobs, raising our families, playing Xbox, and watching The Voice. Yes, you know it. Again, a major reason why the vote is a weak instrument in making sure what goes on politically in our country doesn't get out of control.

Best way to do it, actually, is to get involved at the local level, or at least get online to sign some petitions. Some of the top websites for civic engagement are Thunderclap, Act.Ly, Causes, Citizinvestor, and Avaaz. But be careful, it's very easy to set up a petition on most of these sites, and some of the petitions may just be jokes or unworthy causes. You be the judge.

I am probably one of the few who does watch CSPAN religiously. Certainly do. I watch five minutes and it puts me right to sleep every night. Great for my insomnia.

Every Bill which shall have passed the House of Representatives and the Senate, shall, before it becomes a Law, be presented to the President of the United States; If he approves, he shall sign it, but if

not he shall return it, with his Objections to that House in which it shall have originated, who shall enter the Objections at large on their Journal, and proceed to reconsider it. If after such Reconsideration two thirds of that House shall agree to pass the Bill, it shall be sent, together with the Objections, to the other House, by which it shall likewise be reconsidered, and if approved by two thirds of that House, it shall become a Law. But in all such Cases the Votes of both Houses shall be determined by Yeas and Nays, and the Names of the Persons voting for and against the Bill shall be entered on the Journal of each House respectively. If any Bill shall not be returned by the President within ten Days (Sundays excepted) after it shall have been presented to him, the Same shall be a Law, in like Manner as if he had signed it, unless the Congress by their Adjournment prevent its Return, in which Case it shall not be a Law.

"Blub, glub, glub . . ." Sorry, you took way too much time with this one. I was into some serious REM there.

Anyway, this is how a bill becomes a law. If you need to know more about this, go watch School House Rock (yes, I'm a fan). What are you doing reading this for anyway? Didn't you pay attention all those Saturday mornings? Bad cartoon watcher! Bad! (I'm very aware of Nickelodeon, TV Land, MeTV, etc. No excuses.) Onward ….

Every Order, Resolution, or Vote to which the Concurrence of the Senate and House of Representatives may be necessary (except on a question of Adjournment) shall be presented to the President of the United States; and before the Same shall take Effect, shall be approved by him, or being disapproved by him, shall be repassed by two thirds of the Senate and House of Representatives, according to the Rules and Limitations prescribed in the Case of a Bill.

This is the famous **Presentment Clause** you're all familiar with . . . And it's just about . . .

(Author looking at all the blank faces.)

No? I am surprised. You've heard of the Beatles? Well then, what is wrong with you people? This one is on the same level of popularity. Gesh, get a clue.

Bottom line, the clause makes sure that the president gets involved in making bills. Mr. Executive in charge, goin' large, like a boss …. OK!

Section 8: Powers of Congress

The Congress shall have power to lay and collect taxes, duties, imposts and excises, to pay the debts and provide for the common defense and general welfare of the United States; but all duties, imposts and excises shall be uniform throughout the United States;

Herein are expressed explicit and implicit powers; implied, such as drafting people to raise an army. There are also inherent powers that are not granted by the Constitution, such as regulating immigration.
One of the most important powers given Congress is the power to tax. This may seem like a bad thing at any time in history. Mention "taxation" and it will touch a raw nerve. However, there is a downside to Congress not being able to tax. Under the Articles of Confederation, Congress did not have the authority to collect taxes; therefore, it could only ask the states nicely for funds, which did not work. Therefore, the nation went deep into debt. So like it or not, we do not have much of a choice. Congress must tax because few are volunteering to fund public roads, schools, and protection on their own.

Congress, as we know, also has the power to spend. To many this is a moot point, but it must be done to **"provide for the common Defense and general Welfare of the United States."** Difficult to do without raising funds. However, along with raising funds, it may even regulate economic activity as it did in 1984 when it held back highway funding for states that did not raise the drinking age to twenty-one (How 'bout that! Bet you didn't know your govt. is an extortionist, he said jokingly looking around for agents).

You can see here the obvious need for separation of powers, term limits, impeachment or dismissal from office, and so on. Keeping power under control is an essential element of the Constitution, once again.

According to **Section 8**, when Congress is taxing citizens with "**duties, imposts, and excises**" it must do so in a uniform fashion. Imagine the complexity and confusion and the number of miffed citizens if done otherwise.

To borrow money on the credit of the United States;

Another thing Congress can do is borrow money, much to your chagrin, I know. Moreover, there is no set limit to the amount borrowed, as we know. However, if there were a set limit or dollar figure laid down by the Founding Fathers, it would have to be Patrick Jane-like in nature, a literal seeing into the future.

As you contemplate this point, you truly get to see not only the malleable nature of the Constitution and the brilliance of those who composed it, but the difficulties as well. Here was a group of men who had to consider the fact that this document may just last, if fortunate, a couple hundred years or so. And yes, there were Founding Fathers who believed that the document would not last, nor were they certain about the country itself lasting very long.

To regulate commerce with foreign nations, and among the several states, and with the Indian tribes;

Now we get to the Commerce Clause. From the end of the 19th century into the 20th, the Supreme Court worked to limit Congress's ability to regulate the economy. Then beginning in the 1930s and continuing several decades, The Supreme Court flip-flopped (See, it's not only politicians who do so).

In 1937, the Supreme Court began to support the New Deal and its greater regulating of the economy. Some say this happened because Franklin Roosevelt, out of frustration with the Court's previous rulings, filled the Court with his own nominees. But the 1930s were a time of unrest economically and internationally, and within this great uncertainty, the Supreme Court may have just been relinquishing power to a much needed leader, as many have turned to leaders in dire times throughout history.

Now keeping in mind our theme of change and adaptation, the Court changed directions again with decisions in 1995 and 2000. Allegedly, the Supreme Court said that there was not a sufficient connection to interstate commerce when Congress passed a law creating gun-free school zones and the Violence Against Women Act.

And to this you say WHAT?!

How or why these issues should be connected to commerce is beyond me. I suppose I should read up on it, but I have better things to do with my time, like feed my family. Anyway, for some reason these concerns were brought before the Court under the Commerce Clause. Maybe I'm missing something here, but just call me an old knucklehead who can't figure out the greater minds of Court and Congress.

Next we have the clause which states that Congress should "**establish a uniform Rule of Naturalization, and uniform Laws on the subject of Bankruptcies throughout the United States.**"

This passage gives Congress the power to enact laws governing immigration and naturalization. However, like in any young country, there were big mistakes made along the way because of this power, such as the Chinese Exclusion Act (1882) which was the first federal law that restricted immigration based on race.

But what's interesting about immigration is something many are not specifically aware of that is stated in the **5th Amendment.** Here one will find the Due Process Clause, which protects even illegal immigrants. Because of this clause, the INS cannot indefinitely detain deportable immigrants who cannot get back to their countries. There are other inherent rights of illegals that are protected by the Constitution, but we'll get to those as we go.

Congress, according to **Article 8**, can also "**coin Money, regulate the Value thereof, and of foreign Coin, and fix the Standard of Weights and Measures.**" Enough said about that. Let's get to the more interesting stuff. **Counterfeiting.**

To provide for the punishment of counterfeiting the securities and current coin of the United States;

The States can't coin money (even though they used to under the Articles of Confederation, which has added considerably to the portfolios of coin collectors) and neither can you. But I know some of you have over the years. I've seen your counterfeit stocks, bonds, paper money, and coins. Some of it was very impressive. However, keep in mind the punishment if you continue to do so.

"Under federal law, counterfeiting is a class C felony, punishable by up to 12 years in prison and/or a fine of as much as $250,000. State laws also establish penalties for counterfeiting." (http://law.jrank.org/)

It doesn't specifically say how much you need to produce or what amount of coins, paper money, and so on, or if it gets worse for you the more you counterfeit, and, once again, I suppose I could look this up but . . . Well, you know. Anyway, the best thing to do here is to just say no to all your buddies who suggest doing so, even if the stock market is about to crash and government bailouts are dysfunctional.

Section 8 also tells us citizens that the Congress can **"establish Post Offices and post Roads."** Not a lot here, so let's move on.

Congress should also—as many know but may not know the source of the "why." **"Promote the Progress of Science and useful Arts, by securing for a limited Time for Authors and investors the exclusive Right of their respective writings and Discoveries."**

All this, of course, is to promote innovation and creativity, which Congress has done a good job of, for the majority of winners of The Nobel Prize come from the United States. For example, as of 2008, The Nobel, a Swedish prize, has been awarded to 309 Americans. Second in line is the United Kingdom with 114; third is Germany with 101; fourth is France with 57.

But don't think that the total for the US is considerable merely because the populace is large, for if you look at some other large countries like Japan (16), China (3) and India (8), you can see the numbers are way down by comparison. So even though many Americans complain that school years in this country are too short in comparison to many other countries all that free time does lend itself to the incubation of considerable creative thought. Good job, Congress!

To constitute tribunals inferior to the Supreme Court;

Section 8 allows Congress to create courts under the Supreme Court, such as appellate and federal district courts. We'll get more into all this Court stuff in **Article III.**

Congress can also **"define and punish Piracies and Felonies on the high Seas, and Offences against the Law of Nations."** Here we see a rare occasion when Congress can enact criminal laws. Congress will also respect international law, in some respects, but it also has the power to process those who encroach upon international law according to its own standards and desires.

Congress can also **"declare War, grant Letters of Marque and Reprisal, and make Rules concerning Captures on Land and Water."**

According to this statement, Congress declares war and then the president makes the military decisions. But Congress rarely declares war; it's usually the president. And sometimes neither declares war, at least officially, such is the case with the Korean War and Vietnam War. This is why the **War Powers Act** was passed in **1973**, thus limiting the president's power to declare war and putting Congress back in control. However, many presidents have simply ignored the act as the Supreme Court was unwilling to rule in these cases. And ain't that politics!

Letters of marquee and reprisal deal with attacking an enemy ship and not being punished as a Captain Jack type character (that's a pirate for you landlubbers). Not applicable in this day 'n' age. We don't make many captures on sea any more. If we do, I'll go back and rewrite this section.

Moving on.

To raise and support Armies, but no Appropriation of Money to that Use shall be for a longer Term than two Years; to provide and maintain a Navy; to make Rules for the Government and Regulation of the land and naval Forces; to provide for the calling forth the Militia to execute the Laws of the Union, suppress Insurrections and repel invasions;

Basically?

The Colonists hated standing armies or regulars like the Red Coats. Remember the Boston Massacre? Yes, a standing army that killed five colonists. During these times, of course, standing armies were placed amongst the colonists without their say, so memories die hard. Another reason for term limits. But at the same time, Congress knew that people are people not angels, or at least of the benevolent variety. It's the fallen angel types that Congress was guarding against when they talked about suppressing **"Insurrections and repel invasions."** Our Militia, now the National Guard, is to be called forth in these times of need.

OK, let's talk US Capitol. What's that mean? Here, read this.

Article II is about one-third the length of **Article I**. Why? Well, some may say to give the president more power or flexibility, meaning, less said about what you can and cannot do the more you can do. But it also may have to do with the fact that the president is only the enforcer of laws. "Only?" you say. Well, consider that Congress creates the laws, herein lies greater power thus more controls are required or the reason for a lengthier **Article I**. And of course the president can veto, but that veto can be overridden after the bill has been sent back to Congress and each house passes it into law with a two-thirds majority vote. But even though there is much less copy to **Article II** than **Article I**, the Executive Branch is greater in size by a considerable amount. The executive contains the president and his vice president and cabinet members, but there are also some three million civilian and military employees as well.

Section 1: The President

"The executive Power shall be vested in a President of the United States of America. He shall hold his Office during the Term of four Years, and, together with the Vice-President chosen for the same Term, be elected, as follows:"

OK, so the colonists were a bit touchy about the executive position. Remember that they were just coming out from under the rule of a very much hated monarch in King George III. But at the same time, the Articles of Confederation was opposed because it lacked a strong executive. But then again, some delegates were so afraid of a single executive that they considered two. Could you imagine that? Two people at the helm of the executive branch? Maybe something like an Abigail / John, Nancy / Ronald or Hillary / Bill president? Nah, that would never happen.

Some have felt that the president doesn't have all that much power, our president being kind of like the Queen of England today, just prettier. For instance, Ike Eisenhower felt much more control as a general than president. But because Congress creates laws, and the president only has the weak veto, he is allowed greater leeway than Congress by the Supreme Court. Article II gives the president all executive power. Even the Supreme Court has helped the president in this regard by advocating more times than not that there are certain inherent powers in the presidency not specifically mentioned in the Constitution.

But he needs all the help he can get. Here is what political pundit George Will has to say about the presidency: "Congressional supremacy is . . . a constitutional fact: there is little the president can do if a determined congressional majority opposes it." So maybe the members of the Constitutional Convention knew this and felt for the president by seemingly putting more restrictions on Congress. But we know better, don't we? Then again . . .

In recent history, some say that the power of the presidency has gotten out of hand: Nixon's disregard for protocol in the Watergate scandal; Bush ignoring the majority—public, cabinet, committee—which wanted the U.S. to get out of Iraq—to many an obviously unwinnable war. Former secretary of state James Baker, head of the bipartisan Iraq Study Group, reported in 2006 that "the situation in Iraq is grave and deteriorating" and "U.S. forces seem to be caught in a mission that has no foreseeable end". But even with these power-mongering oversights of the greater good's opinion, the president has little opportunity to really push the envelope, for term limits and impeachment are neigh at hand.

Let's take a look at the responsibility of the president in **waging war, raising tariffs, enacting sanctions** and so on.

Have you ever thought about how responsible the president could or should be in regards to the acts he performs while in office? According to the Supreme Court, the president has "**absolute immunity from damages liability**" for his presidential acts. But even though there appears to be great power in the presidency, term limits, impeachment, and the mere fact that even the president's desires have often been ignored by Congress and the American people, leads one to believe otherwise. But let's move on.

Of course we now know that the president serves a four-year term, and according to the Twenty-second Amendment, he can be re-elected to a second term. However, the framers of the Constitution at one time believed that the president should serve a single term from seven to twenty years!

OK, now onto the sacrosanct and revered office of Vice President. From the dawn of time, men and women (see Nancy Pelosi) have sought this office with great vigor . . .

OK, that's a lie. Here is what Franklin Roosevelt's VP John Garner said about the office: "[it] isn't worth a bucket of spit." OK, so John was a little over the top there. I know he would rather have been VP than head burger flipper at any greasy joint. Well, at least I hope.

But the VP actually doesn't get to do much. The framers of the Constitution didn't put much thought into the role thus the quality of the person filling the position. I guess they didn't think much about assassination. If they had known one of the greatest presidents of all time was going to be shot in the head by an actor while watching a play, they may have reconsidered.

So what does the VP do? He is the president of the Senate, and if you have watched Congress, you will see him--or her someday--sitting behind whoever is speaking at the podium. But don't get excited, the real power of Congress lies in the majority leader. The VP is, after all, to the greatest degree just a figurehead, much to the chagrin of Garner and other VPs (Read about Lyndon Johnson's view of the post, and you will see he was quite in agreement with Garner).

But it is up to the candidate running for president to select a vice president. So what does that mean? Well, think about it. If you were president, would you want someone who is overly ambitious or who outshines you as VP? Maybe someone on the ball, sure, but at least someone of a little duller bulb, shall we say.

Here is an experiment you can run to test this theory. Look at the personalities, intellect, and temperament of former VPs to see if this is true. As a case in point, let me say two words:
Nancy Pelosi. McCain didn't select her just for her pretty face or to fill in the Hillary void.

Each State shall appoint, in such Manner as the Legislature thereof may direct, a Number of Electors, equal to the whole Number of Senators and Representatives to which the State may be entitled in the Congress: but no Senator or Representative, or Person holding an Office of Trust or Profit under the United States, shall be appointed an Elector.

OK, out of all the articles, this section is one of the most complicated. Here we are dealing with the Electoral College. When dealing with this issue, some may simply say, "Good luck."

Consider that those at the Constitutional Convention were some of our best and brightest. They were attempting to put together a "law of the land" that was good for the many not the few. However, these few were smart, privileged, and of the minority, actually, those spoken of as "men" in Jefferson's statement "All *men* are created equal; . . . endowed by their Creator with certain unalienable rights; . . . life, liberty, and the pursuit of happiness. . ." Here he was talking about white-male landowners, not women, minorities or even most white men.

And there is always a problem when smart guys get together to determine the welfare of the majority. That's right, the problem entails the human weaknesses of pride and control. The same problem Plato encountered in his Republic; he attempted to conjure the ideal society. He felt that this society should consist of three parties: "producers (craftsmen, farmers, artisans, etc.), auxiliaries (warriors), and guardians (rulers). Rulers must rule, auxiliaries must uphold rulers' convictions, and producers must limit themselves to exercising whatever skills nature granted them" (Spark Notes).

Now, do not think that these Founding Smart Guys were not aware of Plato or John Lock or other smart guys throughout history who spoke of sociopolitical issues, for they were. Why do I bring this up now? Well, consider that the Constitution does not speak of the general populace's right to vote. The Constitutional delegates didn't even define a national standard for voter eligibility or participation in presidential elections nor did they trust the "auxiliaries" and "producers." They felt that the general populace would not make an informed choice. I see many of you nodding your heads in the affirmative.

But there were some smart guys-thank heavens!-who felt for the people, thus the Electoral College, a compromise. But even though the college exists, the power of the vote still resides in the state not the people.

For example, the 2000 debacle . . . err, presidential election, or Hanging Chad fiasco, points out the power of the states in determining the presidential election. Remember all that hand counting in Florida? Well, after the Florida Supreme Court ordered the hand re-count, the U.S. Supreme Court played its trump card and said that according to the Constitution the state could step in at any time (legislatures) and choose the electors even though the state had initially allowed the people to do so. But according to the U.S. Supreme court, all that hand counting ended up treating voters differently and that doing so violated the 14th Amendment.

So even though most states let the popular vote (the people) elect the electors (remember, you are not *directly* electing the president), the legislature could usurp that power and elect the president if any state decides to do so.

Shocking? For some, I am sure. But that is why you are reading this. And remember, if you don't learn this stuff and learn it well, you will be asked to leave the country. OK, my rule, but I think something close to this should be endorsed so that more make better-informed decisions when electing government officials.

But how does the Electoral College work?

Bottom line, you as average Joe or Jane citizen *have no Constitutional right to vote*. Contrary to all those celebrities who tell you otherwise. It's really a big sham, isn't it? Well, I am sorry but you're just gonna have to open your eyes and smell the bureaucracy or is that nostrils? Anyway ...

So anyway, the framers never got the Electoral College to work as they envisioned. They were hoping that these electors (none allowed to be from Congress) would make the best decisions when elected do so. But how do they get elected? Well, that is a loaded question, Joe and Jane citizen.

But before we get into that, just *who* or *how many* does an electoral vote represent? For example, at this time New York has 31 electoral votes. But what number of citizens does that actually represent? Well, in New York, one electoral vote represents 550,000 citizens; however, that same single vote in South Dakota, a much smaller state population, represents 232,000 people. Ah ha! You say. Now you see why a candidate can win more states than his opponent and still loose, as my daughter pointed out in the 2008 election. "But Dad, McCain has more states!" she exclaimed. "Yes, dear," said dad, "but they're all in the Mid-West where most of the people in the U.S. *don't* live." Or even win the popular vote but lose in the Electoral College because the candidate won too many states with low electoral votes which has happened four times.

Now this creates another issue. Do you as a candidate just campaign in states like, say, New York, Texas, and California ignoring the smaller states? No, not a good policy. Why? Well, because winning the Electoral College requires a majority of electoral votes, so you need more than just the big states. Also, consider that if a candidate focuses only on large states and loses in those states, his chance for election will be over quickly. But some say that no Electoral College means candidates would ignore regional issues and focus on national issues. Nevertheless, it is all speculation. We will know better when or if changes are made.

The Electors shall meet in their respective States, and vote by Ballot for two persons, of whom one at least shall not lie an Inhabitant of the same State with themselves. And they shall make a List of all the Persons voted for, and of the Number of Votes for each; which List they shall sign and certify, and transmit sealed to the Seat of the Government of the United States, directed to the President of the Senate. The President of the Senate shall, in the Presence of the Senate

and House of Representatives, open all the Certificates, and the Votes shall then be counted. The Person having the greatest Number of Votes shall be the President, if such Number be a Majority of the whole Number of Electors appointed; and if there be more than one who have such Majority, and have an equal Number of Votes, then the House of Representatives shall immediately chuse by Ballot one of them for President; and if no Person have a Majority, then from the five highest on the List the said House shall in like Manner chuse the President. But in chusing the President, the Votes shall be taken by States, the Representation from each State having one Vote; a quorum for this Purpose shall consist of a Member or Members from two-thirds of the States, and a Majority of all the States shall be necessary to a Choice. In every Case, after the Choice of the President, the Person having the greatest Number of Votes of the Electors shall be the Vice President. But if there should remain two or more who have equal Votes, the Senate shall chuse from them by Ballot the Vice-President. (This clause was superseded by the Twelfth Amendment.)

Got all that? OK, let me lend a hand.

The Twelfth Amendment changed this clause because the Constitution was written before the prominence of political parties. There was no safe guard against you winning the presidency and your vice president, the general runner up, ends up being your adversary, like when Jefferson won the presidency while his rival, John Adams, became vice president. Just imagine an Obama / Trump ticket? An interesting predicament.

But with the passage of the Twelfth Amendment, the president and vice president were provided separate balloting procedures. If a candidate did not receive a majority of electoral votes, the House of

Representatives would select the president and / or the Senate the vice president.

Initially, the Electoral College was used as a nominating device. After some time, parties became prominent and individual parties electing respective candidates did the nominating, as they do now, of course. And if you followed the 2016 primaries, you understand the complexities even abuse of the system, which has a tendency to be altered too frequently at a whim. Similar issues have arisen in the general election as well—see the "hanging chad," "fat chad," or "pregnant chad" incident of the 2000 election.

So with the growth of parties, the framer's concept of an independent group of electors ended. But if electors now represent their respective parties, what's the point? Why do we still have the Electoral College? For the original meaning was for electors to vote independent of parties. Now electors are to pledge, at the behest of the Supreme Court even, their votes to their party. Rarely has there been a renegade elector. In the primaries, delegates, as you know, are a different story—some bound, some not.

Now you can see the complexity and, some say, the uselessness of the Electoral College. It does seem odd that electors are not really making a choice being beholden or pledged to their party. And it is also odd that a candidate can win the popular vote but lose in the Electoral College and on and on. There is much more to say about this issue, but I did promise not to go into "boring detail," so I will keep my promise.

The Congress may determine the Time of chusing the Electors, and the Day on which they shall give their Votes; which Day shall be the same throughout the United States.

OK, have you ever thought it odd that we always vote on a Tuesday in November every four years? Coincidence? I think not. By federal statute, we vote the first Tuesday after the first Monday in November every four years, like clockwork. But you have to remember that you and I are not electing the president. There is no such thing as the popular vote. OK, it exists but that is not what gets a president into office.

Now here is something that is "stamp-like" in nature-meaning, it is really just a formality. Once again, according to federal law, electors must cast their vote on the first Monday after the second Wednesday in December. And according to Congress, on January 6th those votes are counted at a joint session (Senate and House) in Congress. Then after the president elect wins again, for remember the Supreme Court has firmly suggested party elegance, the new president is sworn in on January 20th, according to the Twentieth Amendment.

Enough with this Electoral College, on to some new stuff.

No person except a natural born Citizen, or a Citizen of the United States, at the time of the Adoption of this Constitution, shall be eligible to the Office of President; neither shall any Person be eligible to that Office who shall not have attained to the Age of thirty-five Years, and been fourteen Years a Resident within the United States.

OK, so no matter how much you love Antonio Banderas, Selma Hyack, Jacki Chan, Arnold Schwarzenegger et al, no, they cannot be elected U.S. President. You have to be natural born, and at least thirty-five years old and fourteen non-consecutive years as a U.S. resident. Enough said.

In Case of the Removal of the President from Office, or of his Death, Resignation, or Inability to discharge the Powers and Duties of the said Office, the same shall devolve on the Vice President, and the Congress

may by Law provide for the Case of Removal, Death, Resignation or Inability, both of the President and Vice President, declaring what Officer shall then act as President, and such Officer shall act accordingly, until the Disability be removed, or a President shall be elected (This clause has been modified by the twenty-fifth Amendment).

The Twenty-fifth Amendment makes it clear that if the president dies in office, the vice president shall become the president. If the president and vice president cannot fill the office, by federal statute the succession moves to Speaker of the House, president pro tempore of the Senate, and then secretary of state, followed by cabinet members based on chronological date of hire.

Let us move on.

The President shall, at stated Times, receive for his Services, a Compensation, which shall neither be increased nor diminished during the Period for which he shall have been elected, and he shall not receive within that Period any other Emolument from the United States, or any of them.

Do not expect to get rich on a president's salary alone. Of course, now you can make a pretty penny, some $400,000, but nowadays that will pay the bills nicely not set you up as a jet setter. The real money comes later when you write books and make speeches. Former President Clinton has made some $40 million giving speeches since leaving office. "I never had a nickel to my name until I got out of the White House, and now I'm a millionaire, the most favored person for the Washington Republicans" (The Washington Post, February 23, 2007).

Before he enter on the Execution of his Office, he shall take the following Oath or Affirmation: "I do solemnly swear (or affirm) that I

will faithfully execute the Office of President of the United States, and will to the best of my Ability, preserve, protect and defend the Constitution of the United States."

This is one of a president-elect's shining moments. You are the center of attention, people gather to see just you. The ceremony! The atmosphere! Poets writing poems on your behalf. You have not done anything to merit a negative review so far. Ahhh, the pageantry! The honor! The glory! But don't get too excited, you'll get bad press soon enough. Hell, you're the president.

Section 2: Civilian Power over Military, Cabinet, Pardon Power, Appointments

The President shall be Commander in Chief of the Army and Navy of the United States, and of the Militia of the several States, when called into the actual Service of the United States; he may require the Opinion, in writing, of the principal Officer in each of the executive Departments, upon any subject relating to the Duties of their respective Offices, and he shall have Power to Grant Reprieves and Pardons for Offenses against the United States, except in Cases of Impeachment.

On occasion, I am sure you have seen other leaders of countries or presidents wearing a general's uniform. This does not bode well for the country at hand: Idi Amin, Saddam Hussein, Fidel Castro, Hitler. You get the point. Moreover, this is something that those of the Constitutional Convention strongly opposed. The Commander-in-Chief of the United States military is to be a civilian, for a purpose. Checks and balances at work once again.

What does this mean?

It means that the president is commander-in-chief of the armed forces, but Congress has constitutionally been given the power to declare war- to raise and support armies. However, in recent history, as you are probably aware, presidents have sent soldiers into war without the consent or involvement of Congress. Because of this, and mostly due to the lengthy Korean and Vietnam campaigns, Congress established the War Powers Act. Basically, the president cannot deploy troops for more than sixty days without Congressional approval. However, there is an inherent problem here too. What of the time and expense, never mind the emotional drain, of sending troops for two months who then have to be withdrawn because of Congressional say so.

And even though there is Constitutional law, it is not always adhered to. For example, here is what George H. W. Bush had to say about Congressional approval in sending troops into the Persian Gulf: "I didn't have to get permission from some old goat in the United States Congress to kick Saddam Hussein out of Kuwait." Here we have certainly discovered one important point. In retrospect, regarding all that George W. has said and done, we can see that the apple does not fall far from the tree.

Let us not forget the executive departments or the president's cabinet. The big four being Secretary of State, Secretary of the Treasury, Secretary of Defense, and the Attorney General. The importance of the Cabinet has varied by president over the years. In recent years, the president has acted through the Executive Office of the President or the National Security Council rather than through the Cabinet. This has brought previously less important cabinet members to greater prominence. However, some presidents, like Franklin D. Roosevelt, did not pay much heed to his cabinet. Others have. There may be a preference for acting through the EOP over that of the Cabinet because most appointees in the EOP don't have to be approved through the Senate. Ah, but I go into too much detail.

Let's move on.

He shall have Power, by and with the Advice and Consent of the Senate, to make Treaties, provided two thirds of the Senators present concur; and he shall nominate, and by and with the Advice and Consent of the Senate, shall appoint Ambassadors, other public Ministers and Consuls, Judges of the supreme Court, and all other Officers of the United States, whose Appointments are not herein otherwise provided for, and which shall be established by Law: but the Congress may by Law vest the Appointment of such inferior Officers, as they think proper, in the President alone, in the Courts of Law, or in the Heads of Departments.

The president negotiates treaties with other countries; however, these treaties do not become binding until ratified by a two-thirds vote in the Senate. But once again there are grey areas. Presidents have used "executive agreements" (An agreement made between the executive branch of the U.S. government and a foreign government without ratification by the Senate) much to the chagrin of the Senate, which is left out of the process. Another problem concerns the presidential interpretation or refusal to enforce a treaty. Once again, points lending themselves to the fact that the Constitution is not cast in stone is interpretive and depends a great deal on individual (president) and collective (Congress) interpretation.

You may be thinking that these executive agreements can be dangerous when a president is making decisions sans any checks made by Congress. And there have been times when these secret agreements created considerable controversy, such as at Alta (site of an Allied conference attended by Franklin D. Roosevelt, Winston Churchill, and Joseph Stalin in February 1945) and the bombing of Cambodia and Laos. But considering the red tap involved in making decisions with Congress involved or the example of the convoluted and limiting nature of the failed League of Nations, when speed in decision making is essential, there is reason to support presidential autonomy. But this is an issue that requires a lot of monitoring and analysis by those better suited than me, your friendly neighborhood civil servant.

On with the show.

According to the Constitution, the president makes appointments that are subject to the consent of the Senate. Kind of. In choosing his cabinet, the president may be left unto his own, unofficially. However, when choosing judges, who serve for life, it might behoove all parties involved that others (the Senate) get involved.

Some judges have been disallowed from judgeship because of political differences; but having the Senate step in here is not all bad, considering that judges serve for life. You might want a second, third, fourth . . . one-hundredth or more opinion in such a case, yes?

The President shall have Power to fill up all Vacancies that may happen during the Recess of the Senate, by granting Commissions which shall expire at the End of their next Session.

Here, the president can assign individuals to fill vacancies while the Senate is in recess. Not that the new kid in the House is then working alone while all the other Senators are on break. No. The president uses the clause to bypass a deadlock with the Senate over a controversial nominee. However, when Congress is back in session, it must approve the appointee by the end of the next session. In addition, even though an appointee may not be immediately ousted, attempting to sneak in an unwanted or controversial official by the president does not encourage good relations between the commander-in-chief and Congress.

Have presidents used this clause often? You, be the judge. Ronald Regan made 232 recess appointments; George H. W. Bush made 78; George W. Bush 171.

Section 3: State of the Union, Convening Congress

He shall from time to time give to the Congress Information of the State of the Union, and recommend to their Consideration such Measures as he shall judge necessary and expedient; he may, on extraordinary Occasions, convene both Houses, or either of them, and in Case of Disagreement between them, with Respect to the Time of Adjournment, he may adjourn them to such Time as he shall think proper; he shall receive Ambassadors and other public Ministers; he shall take Care that the Laws be faithfully executed, and shall Commission all the Officers of the United States.

Traditionally, the president gives his state of the union address each January before Congress begins a joint session that highlights his legislative program for the year to come.

As stated before, the president is the sole representative of the United States when dealing with other countries. No one can usurp this power.

This clause also reveals the president's power as enforcer of the laws laid out by Congress: "**he shall take Care that the Laws be faithfully executed.**" He has at his command not only the military but also the "executive order" (Regulations issued by the President, provided they are based either on his constitutional powers or laws passed by Congress, they have the force of law) which is law-like in nature until rescinded by Congress, the courts, or a future president. Some examples of this power are the sending of the National Guard in times of internal unrest or the banning of segregation in the military. But if the order is found to be unconstitutional by Congress or by the next president, if the order is still in effect, it can be nullified.

How often have presidents used the executive order? Since 1789, over 15,000 times.

Section 4 - Disqualification

The President, Vice President and all civil Officers of the United States, shall be removed from Office on Impeachment for, and Conviction of, Treason, Bribery, or other high Crimes and Misdemeanors.

The House of Representatives has the power to impeach while the Senate tries the accused. However, impeachment is not, contrary to popular misinterpretation, the conviction of an individual but merely the charge of an offense.

Impeachment, which is not subject to judicial review, applies to the executive branch and judicial but not to Congress. It is not a criminal proceeding and is restricted to the removal from office.

The majority of those impeached over the years have been judges (13). Only three presidents have been impeached. Two presidents, Andrew Johnson and Bill Clinton, were acquitted, meaning that Congress did not reach a two-thirds majority for removal from office. One president, Richard Nixon, avoided impeachment by resigning. Enough said.

The People's U.S. Constitution: Article III, The Judicial Branch

OK, so there is not much here. We have gone from Article I with 10 sections to Article II with 5 sections down to Article III with 3 sections. The significance? Maybe those at the Constitutional Convention were getting more and more tired of convening. Have you ever convened? It is taxing. Oh, sorry, that's Article I.

Anyway, in recent history, the Supreme Court believes that Article III gives it the power to determine whether Congress or the Executive are doing anything unconstitutional. Now since the convention was composed of Congressmen (remember that the governing document previous was the Articles of Confederation which did not deal with the executive or judicial), consider their situation. Would you be greatly interested in writing a lot about limiting your own powers or having your laws interpreted? Laws you just pretty much knew how they should be interpreted. Now that may seem a bit infantile, but we are talking human beings, and even smart ones at the head of the class have basic human emotions, wants, needs. For more on this, go back to Article II concerning emotional outbreaks and how Congress deals with them. I digress.

However, this interpreting of the Constitution has certainly, as you probably know, been one of the most volatile issues in American government, so let us get into it, shall we?

Section 1: Judicial Powers

The judicial Power of the United States, shall be vested in one Supreme Court, and in such inferior Courts as the Congress may from time to

time ordain and establish. The Judges, both of the supreme and inferior Courts, shall hold their Offices during good Behavior, and shall, at stated Times, receive for their Services a Compensation which shall not be diminished during their Continuance in Office.

OK, this "judicial power," what is it? The Founding Smart Guys did not really know because, as I said above, this was all new. There was no national judicial power before the U.S. Constitution. And since this was new, there was not much to say, as for instance, there was to say about the Congressional Branch, as you know.

Moreover, there probably was not as much to say because some (like Alexander Hamilton-one of the chief brains behind our new government) said that the judicial was the "least dangerous" branch of government. The reason being that it could only interpret law not establish it as Congress can or enforce as the Executive. However, some say this is not true because these unelected judges have the power to overturn the decisions of elected officials.

So does the power to interpret law solely lie within the judicial? Kind of. If you listen to the Supreme Court and the way it has interpreted law and how people have reacted to those interpretations, well then, the answer is yes. However, over the years, on occasion states have had the power to declare the acts of Congress unconstitutional and even the president has stepped in and put in his two cents. But of course, it is actually the people who have the final say in accepting or rejecting changes to the Constitution through the amendment. But we know doing so is an arduous process and of the hundreds of proposed amendments only 27 have passed, so far.

Now, regarding the establishment of courts, only Congress has the power to do so. Today we have the federal district courts where trial cases are heard, U.S. appellate that hear the first level of appeals in the federal system, up to the Supreme Court where final appeals are heard.

But what about job requirements? The Constitution actually says nothing about this. Unlike Congress or the presidency, there are no age limits or length of citizenship requirements. In addition, lawyers before 1957 actually trained through apprentices. They had no law degrees. And you don't even need to practice law or to have been a lawyer to be a judge; however, up to this point, all judges have been lawyers.

If you are into having serious time off or time off like a European employee become a judge. The Court's term begins in October and ends in June. That is a three-month vacation. Interestingly enough, the court begins working on its most controversial issues in June. Got something you don't want to do? Put it off until June and you may not have to deal with it.

And what do we know of the judges and their duties? The Constitution only mentions the chief justice, he or she who is in charge of the entire judicial branch not just the Supreme Court. (Stand by for more on this in the next clause.) Judges work in considerable isolation, not even seeing other judges that often, but they have clerks do much of the administrative work, sorting through thousands of petitions and summarizing them. They even help judges write out their opinions. As a judge, you don't have to deal with the public, answer to constituents, raise money for campaigning or re-election, and you get a nice and steady, low six-figure salary for life, as well as all the other perks, of course. Not a bad gig, if you can get it.

Now what of this "good behavior" mentioned in this section? Is it just me or does this phrase stand out as a bit odd? Let's see why it's there in the first place.

Well, consider that judges are assigned not elected "of the people, by the people, and for the people." Here the "majority rule" concept of our republic gets dogged. And on top of all that these judges serve for life. The only way this life term can end is through death, of course, resignation or impeachment. However, today many think that judges should have term limits.

However, since constitutionally there are no specifics as to how judges should interpret or apply law, what's a judge to do? Well, you can basically, like in many political situations, go one of two ways: you can restrain yourself or get into it. You can go with set precedents or apply more personal interpretations of laws and precedents. You can interpret the Constitution narrowly or broadly. And until it's specifically put into the Constitution (don't hold your breath), that's how judges do it and will continue to do so.

But herein lies a problem too, for interpretation is often so subjective. Look at the Bible. Followers of Christ or Christians wrote the Bible. Some say that one should just follow its tenants or, more specifically, the Ten Commandments. However, if this were so easy to do, we would only have one Christian church and not the many offshoots and sects that exist, 600 I believe is the number. That's a lot of subjective interpretation.

So there is a large gray area here; for even those traditionalists who want to stick to original meaning, often times there's no original meaning to go to. Merely following the Constitution in many cases of law just will not fly because there is not enough written to lead one to a Constitution-bound decision. Even the framers often disagreed on interpretation.

Maybe John Hart Ely, author of *Democracy and Distrust*, says it best when he says that if it is not stated clearly in the Constitution, let majority rule. Amen.

Section 2 - Trial by Jury, Original Jurisdiction, Jury Trials

The judicial Power shall extend to all Cases, in Law and Equity, arising under this Constitution, the Laws of the United States, and Treaties made, or which shall be made, under their Authority; to all Cases affecting Ambassadors, other public Ministers and Consuls; to all Cases of admiralty and maritime Jurisdiction; to Controversies to which the United States shall be a Party; to Controversies between two or more States; between a State and Citizens of another State; between Citizens of different States; between Citizens of the same State claiming Lands under Grants of different States, and between a State, or the Citizens thereof, and foreign States, Citizens or Subjects.

Initially, we see that the federal Supreme Court can hear cases regarding the Constitution, U.S. law, and treaties with foreign nations. You will notice an important point here that the federal courts also have jurisdiction over "Controversies between two states." This was written so that prejudice between states is avoided in a case of law with the Supreme Court riding shotgun.

Believe it or not, the federal courts do not hear hypothetical cases. For instance, if you felt you might be in a case to be sued by someone, you cannot go to federal court with a "suppose this were to happen" case. You would have to get advice from an attorney and do what was necessary to prevent a lawsuit and take it from there. The Supreme Court can only hear actual cases. It can also not just give advice, this working along the same lines as the court having to deal with a literal case and not mere theory or conjecture.

So if you're thinking of filing a hypothetical case regarding a possible defamation of character because you suspect your wife is telling your friends that you're watching a 24 DVD set titled The Westminster Dog Show, a Retrospective and NOT Monday Night Football . . . Well, sorry, there is nothing the Supreme Court can do. But I advise you get over to a football buddy's house on Monday Night and watch the damn dog and pony show on Tuesdays. Actually, I prefer Wednesdays. But your choice.

In all Cases affecting Ambassadors, other public Ministers and Consuls, and those in which a State shall be Party, the Supreme Court shall have original Jurisdiction. In all the other Cases before mentioned, the Supreme Court shall have appellate Jurisdiction, both as to Law and Fact, with such Exceptions, and under such Regulations as the Congress shall make.

OK, this gets a little muddled, but it really comes down to the Supreme Court being able to change "appellate jurisdiction," appeals from lower courts (as to which ones it hears), but its Constitutional or "original jurisdiction" can only be changed through amendments.

Over the last century, Congress has slowly gotten rid of appeals from the lower courts. And why not? Consider the growth in population from the 18th to the 20th-21st century. The Supreme Court gets thousands and thousands of petitions a year. That is a lot of work for nine judges, so only about 10% of the cases submitted are accepted.

But there are appellate cases that may need to be heard by the Supreme Court that Congress deems restrictive, such as school prayer, abortion, and criminal procedure. However, Congress has yet to restrict appellate jurisdiction regarding these issues even though the temptation to do so is there.

The Trial of all Crimes, except in Cases of Impeachment, shall be by Jury; and such Trial shall be held in the State where the said Crimes shall have been committed; but when not committed within any State, the Trial shall be at such Place or Places as the Congress may by Law have directed.

Here is a civil liberty expressed specifically in the Constitution not the Bill of Rights. Juries were primary to the framers and are mentioned four times. But how fair are juries? That is a loaded question and one that will be dealt with when we get to the 5th, 6th, and 7th amendments. However, I can tell you from personal experience that not only are juries not ideal they are considerably problematic.

Section 3: Treason

Treason against the United States, shall consist only in levying War against them, or in adhering to their Enemies, giving them Aid and Comfort. No Person shall be convicted of Treason unless on the

Testimony of two Witnesses to the same overt Act, or on Confession in open Court.

The Congress shall have power to declare the Punishment of Treason, but no Attainder of Treason shall work Corruption of Blood, or Forfeiture except during the Life of the Person attainted.

It used to be back in the Mother Country-England in the good old days-that if you spoke poorly of Her, regardless of what you said, this was construed as treasonous. To avoid such a bash of civil liberties, the Constitution requires a high standard of proof; therefore, convictions of treason in the U.S. have been infrequent.

However, even with the implied care of protecting the innocent, years after the Rosenberg Case in which Julius and his wife Ethel were put to death for espionage during WWII (leaking atomic secrets to the Soviet Union), it was discovered that Ethel was only a minor accomplice. No law, of course, is perfect.

The People's U.S. Constitution: Article IV, The States

In the old pre-Constitutional days, states sometimes treated each other more like individual countries than they did United States, so therefore, Article IV. After it was written, even if there were disagreements between states, Article IV required them to acknowledge and accept the laws.

Section 1: Each State to Honor all others

Full Faith and Credit shall be given in each State to the public Acts, Records, and judicial Proceedings of every other State. And the Congress may by general Laws prescribe the Manner in which such Acts, Records and Proceedings shall be proved, and the Effect thereof.

Regarding this clause, a recent most controversial issue entailed the definition of marriage. This issue has specifically come to the forefront after demonstrations that turned violent in Los Angeles regarding Proposition 8: how the state defines marriage. However, no matter how you slice it, there appears to be no happy medium for the two sides in this battle. Regardless, it is up to each state to handle this or any issue on its own, and other states must respect with good faith giving credit where it's due that these decisions are just for said state. That being said, as you know, in 2015, the Court made seam sex marriage legal in all 50 states, thus the constant flux and battle between state and federal influence. You can also look to how states are taking the federal order of refugee immigration, how many are suing or going to court over not desiring to be forced to comply. On and on it goes.

In 1996, Congress passed the Defense of Marriage Act that defined marriage as being between a woman and a man. This allowed states to refuse to recognize same-sex marriage couples from other states. However, some gay-rights activists said that according to the 14th Amendment guarantee of equal protection of laws, the DOMA Act is unconstitutional.

The Constitution is supposed to allow states sovereignty where the Fed is not invoked. However, even though the Fed has tried in the past to usurp State power (the Affordable Care Act is another such instance, where 20 states brought lawsuits against the Fed) states struggle to maintain authority over important political decisions.

Section 2: State citizens, Extradition

The Citizens of each State shall be entitled to all Privileges and Immunities of Citizens in the several States.

Basically, this clause disallows discrimination of citizens of other states. For example, if you teach in one state and then move to another, you can teach there, even though you may be required by the hiring state to be recertified. But the Court hasn't said much about this clause, so let's move on.

A Person charged in any State with Treason, Felony, or other Crime, who shall flee from Justice, and be found in another State, shall on demand of the executive Authority of the State from which he fled, be delivered up, to be removed to the State having Jurisdiction of the Crime.

Here alone we can attest to the arbitrary nature of the Court. Initially, the Supreme Court said that it didn't have the power to require states to extradite or give up a convict to another state (1861). Then in 1987, the Supreme Court said, "Changed our minds" and told governors that they had to give up criminals. Such is life in the "law of the land."

No Person held to Service or Labour in one State, under the Laws thereof, escaping into another, shall, in Consequence of any Law or Regulation therein, be discharged from such Service or Labour, But shall be delivered up on Claim of the Party to whom such Service or Labour may be due. (This clause superseded by the 13th Amendment.)

Not much here, since it deals with slavery. This clause was made a moot point by the Thirteenth Amendment. Since this is not a history course, if you need more on this, I'm sorry, I'm not supplying.

Let's move on.

Section 3: New States

New States may be admitted by the Congress into this Union; but no new States shall be formed or erected within the Jurisdiction of any other State; nor any State be formed by the Junction of two or more States, or parts of States, without the Consent of the Legislatures of the States concerned as well as of the Congress.

Not much chance of this happening these days, unless Texas or California would like to trim down a bit. But little did you know this has been done before: for example, Vermont from New York (now you know why there's so many Yankee fans in Vermont!), Maine from

Massachusetts, and Tennessee from North Carolina. And you know about West Virginia, right? It desired to stay in the Union, and after the Civil War Virginia agreed to the split.

Did you know that the District of Colombia wanted to be a state in 1980? I certainly don't remember this. I guess it wasn't big news in Connecticut at the time. But since Congress has to agree, it never happened. As a matter of fact, the petition for statehood never even got out of the House. Sorry, D.C.

The Congress shall have Power to dispose of and make all needful Rules and Regulations respecting the Territory or other Property belonging to the United States; and nothing in this Constitution shall be so construed as to Prejudice any Claims of the United States, or of any particular State.

Basically, Congress is the big House when it comes to land. It has legislative power over all U.S. property and territory. However, the thank-heavens-for-the-Bill-of-Rights clause applies here. Well, that's my clause, but thank heavens for it. Basically, the BORs steps in and protects the individual from just having to give up land or rights to Congress because it simply says so. And we know how important land is, right? You're familiar with this phrase? "All men have equal rights to life, liberty, and the pursuit of happiness." Well, that happiness part used to be right to property, according to John Locke. A man's home is his castle, yes? You got it.

Let's move on.

Section 4: Republican government

The United States shall guarantee to every State in this Union a Republican Form of Government, and shall protect each of them against Invasion; and on Application of the Legislature, or of the Executive (when the Legislature cannot be convened) against domestic Violence.

Wherever you live, regardless of statehood, you have a right to a "Republican Form of Government." Now, don't get huffy with your "down with the man" attitude there. A republic actually, according to big-brain Founding Father James Madison, is one that gets its power "directly or indirectly from the great body of the people." Is that so bad, Mr. down-with-the-man, man?

But it appears that the framers were all talk no action, for they never specifically defined this "republican government" or who was responsible for enforcing it. But as I said before, all that convening must have gotten to them. And I guess that they figured they'd be dead anyway, why not let our ancestors have a little of the fun and figure out the specifics. "Hell, we've got a new country to get up and running. We damn well don't have all day to work out the specifics" they said with Constitutional angst.

And I'm sure there's more I could say not only about this clause but about this article, but I've got a life to live, and I really don't have all day to give you more specifics, he said with constipated angst (sorry, the truth's out).

The People's U.S. Constitution: Article V, Amendment

The Congress, whenever two thirds of both Houses shall deem it necessary, shall propose Amendments to this Constitution, or, on the Application of the Legislatures of two thirds of the several States, shall call a Convention for proposing Amendments, which, in either Case, shall be valid to all Intents and Purposes, as part of this Constitution, when ratified by the Legislatures of three fourths of the several States, or by Conventions in three fourths thereof, as the one or the other Mode of Ratification may be proposed by the Congress; Provided that no Amendment which may be made prior to the Year One thousand eight hundred and eight shall in any Manner affect the first and fourth Clauses in the Ninth Section of the first Article; and that no State, without its Consent, shall be deprived of its equal Suffrage in the Senate.

So if you remember what the first and fourth Clauses in the Ninth Section of the first Article is all about, you can skip forward. For the rest of you, let's get into it.

To get one of these by Congress, it requires Congress or both Houses to approve an amendment by a two thirds vote, not like under the Articles of Confederation that required a unanimous approval. Basically, under the AOC there would have never been any amendments. As it is with the Constitution, only 27 have been passed out of the thousands and thousands proposed (over 11,000!). Aren't you glad it's difficult to get an amendment passed? I am. Otherwise, I'd be writing to the end of time. You probably know that Congress proposes amendments, but did you know states could too? The framers were, once again, thinking of the people. Not a lot of that going on by government leaders before the colonists moved to the New World, so this void was often on the framer's minds.

But here we're not talking just about proposing. What about getting amendments added to the Constitution?

There were two methods of ratification or the approval of amendments added to the Constitution. States can ratify, but only the 21st amendment has been ratified in this manner. Generally, it's left up to the Legislative branch.

What about getting the ratification of an amendment done? Is there a deadline? or does the amendment after it's been accepted just hang there indefinitely? Well, according to the 18th Amendment, there is a deadline. More on this when we get to amendments.

According to this article, there are three amendments that can't be added to the Constitution. The first two deal with slavery and are moot. The third one dealt with capitalization taxes not being passed before 1808. Another moot point. Remember, way back in the introductory summary I told you these moot points would arise on occasion and that I would not belabor these points. Such is the case here.

Let's move on.

We do have a point in Article V that applies to today that no amendment to the Constitution can deny a state equal representation in the Senate. Big problem today is that larger states like California are represented by two senators while Rhode Island, the smallest state, has the same representation in the Senate. Some, however, believe that Article V refers to governing bodies and not the people. But more on this when we get to amendments.

Let's move on.

The People's U. S. Constitution: Article VI, Debts, Supremacy, and Oaths

According to Article IV, the Constitution is the "supreme law of the land." Here, the point is also made clear that even though the national Constitution is supreme or superior to state power, states are protected under the Constitution. Herein lies the importance of federalism, a political system in which power is shared between the national and state governments.

All Debts contracted and Engagements entered into, before the Adoption of this Constitution, shall be as valid against the United States under this Constitution, as under the Confederation.

Under the Articles of Confederation because of its lack of power over the states, debt was severe. There was also the issue of considerable war debt. And it was at a quiet dinner between friends where Alexander Hamilton agreed with Thomas Jefferson that the new government would take on the war debt for allowing the national capitol to be built on the Potomac River.

This Constitution and the Laws of the United States which shall be made in Pursuance thereof; and all Treaties made, or which shall be made, under the Authority of the United States, shall be the supreme Law of the Land; and the Judges in every State shall be bound thereby, any Thing in the Constitution or Laws of any State to the Contrary notwithstanding.

This is the law that states judges should pledge to uphold The Constitution regardless of conflicts with state laws. It takes no backseat. It is the supreme law of the land. Enough said.

The Senators and Representatives before mentioned, and the Members of the several State Legislatures, and all executive and judicial Officers, both of the United States and of the several States, shall be bound by Oath or Affirmation, to support this Constitution; but no religious Test shall ever be required as a Qualification to any Office or public Trust under the United States.

All state and federal officials must swear to uphold the Constitution, along with military personnel and naturalized citizens. It is interesting to note here the relative lack of familiarity the majority of native-born citizens have with the Constitution. And not only do they not have to pledge to uphold the Constitution but few have more than a cursory knowledge of it. It is this very reason for my extensive people's journey into an understanding and promoting of the same. How are we to make fully informed decisions in voting for political officers, propositions, or for making many decisions regarding city, state, and national issues without a general understanding of this greatest of documents of this greatest of countries?

I rest my case. Your honor?

The People's U.S. Constitution: Article VII, Ratification

The Ratification of the Conventions of nine States, shall be sufficient for the Establishment of this Constitution between the States so ratifying the Same.

Done in Convention by the Unanimous Consent of the States present the Seventeenth Day of September in the Year of our Lord one thousand seven hundred and Eighty seven and of the Independence of the United States of America the Twelfth. In Witness whereof We have hereunto subscribed our Names.
Go Washington - President and deputy from Virginia

New Hampshire - John Langdon, Nicholas Gilman

Massachusetts - Nathaniel Gorham, Rufus King

Connecticut - Wm Saml Johnson, Roger Sherman

New York - Alexander Hamilton

New Jersey - Wil Livingston, David Brearley, Wm Paterson, Jona. Dayton

Pensylvania- B Franklin, Thomas Mifflin, Robt Morris, Geo. Clymer, Thos FitzSimons, Jared Ingersoll, James Wilson, Gouv Morris

Delaware - Geo. Read, Gunning Bedford jun, John Dickinson, Richard Bassett, Jaco. Broom

Maryland - James McHenry, Dan of St Tho Jenifer, Danl Carroll Virginia

- John Blair, James Madison Jr.

North Carolina - Wm Blount, Richd Dobbs Spaight, Hu Williamson

South Carolina - J. Rutledge, Charles Cotesworth Pinckney, Charles Pinckney, Pierce Butler

Georgia - William Few, Abr Baldwin

Attest: William Jackson, Secretary

OK, so there it is. The framers were done. Now they simply began their new government.

You wish!

Or actually, the framers or, should I say, the majority wished. Because only 39 of the 55 delegates signed the Constitution. Many Antifederalists opposed the Constitution until the Bill of Rights was added. And even though the general populace demanded a bill of rights, Alexander Hamilton stated "that the Constitution is itself . . . a bill of rights."

Nine of the thirteen states accepted the Constitution and it was ratified into existence as the current law of the land. And even though the Articles of Confederation required a unanimous say by the states, the framers knew that requiring such would take years, as did the AOC before it was ratified; therefore, nine became the magic number. After much debate and passing of time, eventually New Hampshire became the ninth state to ratify on June 21, 1788.

It may merely have been the signature of the beloved hero, George Washington that did more for the ratification of the Constitution than anything else. It was new. It was all encompassing. And it came on the heels of one of the bloodiest, hard fought battles this country has ever seen, a long fight against an oppressive monarchy that the colonists were all too familiar with. So the fact that it was not accepted by a good many and that there were certainly points to iron out should come as no surprise.

"I wish the Constitution which is offered had been made more perfect, but I sincerely believe it is the best that could be obtained at this time; and . . . a constitutional door is opened for amendment hereafter." George Washington

It is interesting to note the number of people who think history is clean that, for instance, a war between Britain and the American colonies was proposed and everyone just accepted it, buckled down, and fought. However, like with the ratification of the Constitution, there were those who accepted, opposed, and sat on the fence. Nevertheless, the argument goes on. Ben Franklin said it the best when responding to a question as to whether the Constitution was for a republic or a monarchy: "A republic, if you can keep it." So far, so good. But the battle for the rights of the many rages on.

The People's U.S. Constitution: Bill of Rights

OK, The Bill of Rights or the first ten amendments are important and of great interest to most Americans.

Why?

Well, they certainly preserve citizen's rights, but there's more to it than that. You have to remember, the Constitution was written by Americans, certainly, but for the people by a small group of elites who wrote behind closed doors. Not much was known about the document by the average Joe and Jane citizen while it was being written. And even though some of the framers believed that the Constitution is a bill of rights, the "people" still wanted to be sure that their best interest was taken into consideration. Remember, these new Americans had just won a hard-fought freedom and came from the Land of the Monarchs; they didn't want any more of their rights stomped on by powerful courts, dictators, or armies. Enough said.

Amendment I: Freedom of Religion, Press, Expression. Ratified 12/15/1791.

Congress shall make no law respecting an establishment of religion, or prohibiting the free exercise thereof; or abridging the freedom of speech, or of the press; or the right of the people peaceably to assemble, and to petition the Government for a <u>redress </u>**of grievances.**

The **five freedoms** spoken of here- **religion, speech, press, assembly, petition**-enable the "people" to self-govern. As you know, of those amendments in the Bill of Rights, the breech of these freedoms is what you hear about the most and that's because they are at the top of the pecking order. Without these five freedoms, it would be difficult if not impossible for Americans to assert any other rights.

Here's an interesting point about the 1st Amendment; see that first word Congress? Key point; it is the federal government that is limited, not private parties. Your speech, for instance, will be protected in the public arena, not private. If you decide to say something to your boss or your college professor (except for state funded schools, of course), you are not protected by the 1st Amendment. You may be protected if you hold a government job, but it's not failsafe. It's complicated, and like I said, I'm not going to go deep on any of these topics. Just the basics, ma'am.

Let's move on.

Note that I said "federal government." It wasn't until the 14th Amendment in 1897 that the states began to come under the Bill of Rights. There are those who believe that they can say and do as they please without repercussion; however, there may be no absolute. At times there have been those on the Supreme Court who were absolutists, such as Justice Hugo Black. Then again, other justices have been more open to interpretation. And as you know, this is not the first time we've heard of the "subjective" nature of the Court.

The **first freedom** spoken of regards **religion**. The government cannot step in and establish a religion, as a national religion, such as The Church of England. No Church of America, therefore. Also, the government cannot interfere with the expression of religious beliefs, unless, of course, those beliefs inhibit the same of others. And this all sounds fine and dandy, but if you read these two points carefully, and consider the subjective nature of the Court, you can see inherent problems.

But don't think that Americans because of the great liberties inherent in the Constitution and all that talk over the years of freedom this, freedom that, that we are any better than any other people when it comes to doing the right thing. We, like most humans, had to be taught how to behave. We are still learning.

What do I mean?

Before the Constitution, and especially this 1st Amendment, new Americans were, well, pretty much like the old English. The **official religion in the New England colonies** was the **Puritan Church**, and if you decided to sin or do something like not be a Puritan, you were persecuted in the extreme. For example, Quakers were killed just for being Quaker. You could, of course, be killed for being a witch (and why have we never heard of male Wicca, or wizards, being burned at the stake? Yes, its sexual bias but that's another issue for another time), but did you know that if you sinned you'd get whipped or thrown in the stocks? Stripped to the waste, tarred and feathered, and dragged behind a wagon? Remember those movies *The Crucible* and *The Scarlet Letter*? Well, that's what I'm talking about. And the South was not full of good cheer either. They had the fallen variety too. Oh yes! The **established church in the southern colonies, The Church of England**, was also not a protector of individual rights.

Amongst all this talk, I am reminded by a point made by Noam Chomsky. He stated that even though we mail rail in disbelief against what those in power do, we must keep in mind that it's not a failing of those in power that is at root cause for such evil, but rather human nature, so he's basically saying anyone in these positions of power (think Congress) will eventually end up corrupt. Just a little food for thought.

Interestingly enough, many negative issues in American history, like those mentioned above, are not common knowledge. Why? Well, it's mostly the way our high school history text books are written. The main objective is to make patriots, if you didn't know, and if you reveal too many of the negatives of America's past to potential patriots, well then, you're disassembling patriots not assembling. But should all those negatives be left out? Maybe there's a happy medium.

Maybe, just maybe, America isn't perfect, and we've made a few mistakes along the way. What's the problem with talking about these negatives? Or doing so without being called an America hater. Do you hate yourself, brother, sister, mother or father because they've made mistakes? I digress.

So maybe the colonists were not just fearful of the Smart Wise Guys but the common folk as well in obtaining individual rights. So just like the North were not sacrosanct and benevolent in regard to the slavery issue during the Civil War, early Americans were just like other humans who indulged as they deemed fit, unless, of course, limits were applied by a "law of the land."

Now let's get into another important issue, the phrase **"separation of church and state."** This phrase is NOT in the Constitution or, more specifically, in the 1st Amendment. The Supreme Court may have used it, as they did in Everson vs. Board of Education (1947), but it was borrowed from Jefferson when he said in 1802 that the 1st Amendment prohibited states from using religion in legislative concerns and that there should be "a wall of separation between church and state." In regards to this issues, there are two camps or opinions: Accomodationists and Separationists. Either you believe in the strict separation of church and state or you lean in the opposite direction. But there is a choice because of the lack of a specific statement of separation in the Constitution.

But the separation of church and state issue really is about the government not getting involved or sponsoring or advocating religion (one church over another, churches over non-religious groups, or churches in general), especially as regards the young who are more impressionable and open to the effects of proselytizing.

In public situations, especially if initiated by the individual, **the Court has allowed prayer or religious meetings**. For example, if students choose to pray before a game, they may do so. Here it is the student's choice not the schools. However, schools can't make opening prayers or graduation day prayers official, unless, of course, one is in a private school that emphasizes a particular religion. But prayers are allowed in daily legislative sessions because of the absence of children and the belief that adults are less prone to peer pressure or proselytizing. In the case of a proposition that defines marriage, Congress deems it private in that those voting may be religious but there are certainly secular citizens who advocate marriage as being defined as that between a man and woman. Government is not advocating a choice but asking the people to make a decision.

The speech of Americans cannot be abridged. But here speech has often included not just speaking but art, literature, and advertising. But

how does the Supreme Court define "free speech"? According to the Court, there are three types of speech: spoken, spoken along with action, and symbolic like destruction of draft card or the American flag. Certain freedoms of expressions may break laws or are secondary to Congressional concern, such as the religious rites that require the use of illegal drugs or the burning of a draft card where Congress is attempting to raise an army. However, there have been other occasions where symbolic acts have been allowed such as the burning of the American flag to express oneself. However, this symbol is regarded by most states in high standing, and in 2002, all states agreed that they would ratify an amendment to outlaw the burning of the American flag. But today we see it being burned. Again, laws in interpretive flux.

But there are limits to free speech. There are certain types of speech that the 1st Amendment doesn't protect, such as obscenity, defamation, fighting words, and speech that incites illegal action. However, there are always **vague definitions that are open to interpretation**, such as the Court's criteria for obscenity using vague phrases: "contemporary community *standards*," "whether the work depicts or describes, in a *patently offensive way*" and "lacks serious *artistic*, political, or scientific value." What is "standard"? What is "offensive?" What is "art"? Herein lies the challenge the Court has in making decisions.

When the Court makes a decision, it's often not as clear cut as one may think. Motive or why someone has done something is important. For example, in R.A.V. v. St. Paul (1992), the Court disallowed an ordinance that prohibited certain symbols "that arouse anger, alarm, or resentment in others on the basis of race, color, creed, religion, or gender." When a white juvenile put a burning cross on a black family's lawn the Court said that he could do so because he couldn't be punished for the "content of his speech" but he could for arson. However, later the Court set a precedent in Wisconsin v. Mitchell (1993) that "assault" was not expressive conduct.

Some of the Court's decisions may appear odd or unjustified, but it is all in the effort to protect a citizen's Constitutional liberty to express. And the Court is just like any individual who is growing and struggling to get it right.

You've seen the movie ***Clear and Present Danger***? Jack Ryan, played by Harrison Ford, is clearly in danger through most of the movie. No question, right? Congress used this phrase to cover illegal acts not protected under the 1st Amendment. So if you're distributing pamphlets to encourage young men to avoid the draft-especially during war time- organizing to overthrow the government, or leading the KKK in verbally denouncing civil rights laws then you will not be protected under the 1 st Amendment.

Now don't think that youths in school are treated the same as adults in the public arena. Sorry kiddies. You may think it's cool to wear armbands to school protesting the war, but according to the Supreme Court, you can't protest and cause a disturbance in school. You'll have to wait until after class to wear your arm bands. So if you are involved in school sponsored activities, such as student newspapers, class plays and such, you'll have to wait to protest or speak more freely outside of the government-sponsored classroom.

Here's a statement by Robyn Blummer that may shed some light on the issue of free speech, who's offending and who's judging: "Freedom of speech is not about good speech versus bad; it's about who holds the power to decide which is which."

It's the same old story
Everywhere I go,
I get slandered,
Libeled,
I hear words I never heard
In the Bible

According to Paul Simon's song "Keep the Customers Satisfied," the speaker has never heard such libelous, slanderous words in the Bible. Well, he's a rare exception, and unless you're living under a rock, you have too, especially in today's all too promiscuous society. However, how does the Court see spoken (slander) and written (libel) words that defame character?

Interestingly enough, the **1 st Amendment does not protect against defamation or hurting one's character through lies and deceit**. The Court is actually more concerned here about the restrictions on free speech than they are about the good name of celebrities and public officials. It feels that you better have a good case and be able to prove slanderous or libelous allegations, because if you don't, you're going to put a big hurtin' on free speech. So you can say someone's not honest, incompetent, a lay about, but don't start yelling "Scumbag, I'm gonna kill you!" Them's fightin' words. But don't say them or even lesser words like "Fascist" or "racketeer" to a public official like a cop. Here the Court says that such fighting words "have a direct tendency to cause acts of violence," especially, as I said above, if those words are thrown around officials who have direct connection or are in closer approximation to the Court than your average Joe or Jane citizen. But again, in recent years, there's been a push to stand down, people allowed to be slanderous, even get physical with officials. But this has to swing back, as political leanings have over the years (conservative to liberal, liberal to conservative), or it could lead to total anarchy.

When it comes to the five liberties the freedom to **assemble** may seem the most trivial. The framers would agree. They almost left it out. And next to religion, speech, press, even petition, it's not on most people's minds because we do it so often with little worry about being able to do so. And regarding Constitutional law, it's not so much the assembling that's at issue but the when, where, how or that which may disturb the peace, such as blocking traffic, fights, riots, and so on.

And if you don't like what those assembling are doing, did you know you have a veto? Yes, it's called the **heckler's veto**. Actually, as regards the 1st Amendment, the government can shut down a speaker who may cause hecklers to react violently. However, University of Cal, Irvine Law School Dean Erwin Chemerinsky states that speakers have the right to speak. One may demonstrate outside, but allowing people to loudly protest inside would result in few being able to speak at all, of course. Again, none of this is cut and dry and varies from state to state as to how this scenario would be handled.

Amendment II: The Right to Bear Arms. Ratified 12/15/1791.

A well regulated Militia, being necessary to the security of a free State, the right of the people to keep and bear Arms, shall not be infringed.

"The framers recognized that self-government requires the people's access to bullets as well as ballots." Akhil Reed Amar

This amendment came about because the early colonists had more faith in the part-time or citizen army than they did in the regulars or standing army. And why not? There was a bias. They were at the constant behest of a monarch that had a habit of sending standing armies. But why the constant of standing armies? Founding Father and chief author of The Constitution James Madison has this to say:

> A standing military force, with an overgrown Executive will not long be safe companions to liberty. The means of defense against foreign danger, have been always the instruments of tyranny at home. Among the Romans it was a standing maxim to excite a war, whenever a revolt was apprehended. Throughout all Europe, the armies kept up under the pretext of defending, have enslaved the people.

The English had a substantial empire they had to maintain in the colonies, and along with the cost of fighting the French and Spanish in North America, the debt was substantial. In order to pay for this, the colonists were used. But no one will pay against one's will without someone there to make sure they do so; therefore, standing armies.

So the question as to whether the 2nd Amendment should be interpreted as the right of the army or individual to bear arms, the answer is yes. The militia, or the people's army, was used by early American's to keep the invaders at bay. If the main source of concern comes from without, why would the people need the right to bear arms from within? Certainly this self-governing was new and even the threat from one's own government was real-the reason why the colonists left England in the first place-but wouldn't the Constitution's checks and balances keep the new government at bay to protect the average citizen?

Many questions and many concerns, however, the point is moot, for the Constitution is adaptable to current needs, and it is up to the Supreme Court to determine our current needs.

On June 27, 2008 David G. Savage of the Los Angeles Times reported that "Americans have a right to keep a gun at home for self-defense, the Supreme Court ruled today in striking down part of a handgun ban in the District of Columbia. By a 5-4 vote, the court concluded that the 2nd Amendment and its famous right "to keep and bear arms" protect the gun rights of individuals, rather than just a state's right to maintain a militia." However, according to Justice Scalia, "Like most rights, the right secured by the 2nd Amendment is not unlimited.". And many have noted that the 2nd Amendment does not include an unlimited right to own guns. The Supreme Court's decision, however, has certainly opened new avenues to travel down in the future. In addition, D.C. vs. Heller, the 2nd Amendment applies to the states too, not just federal government. So again, one can see the Constitution is not stationary but always in flux.

Amendment III: Quartering of Troops. Ratified 12/15/1791.
No Soldier shall, in time of peace be quartered in any house, without the consent of the Owner, nor in time of war, but in a manner to be prescribed by law.

Now this one's not on the tip of everyone's tongue these days. When was the last time you heard someone complaining about having to quarter troops or heard the subject in the news? Regardless, when the

Constitution was written, it was a big deal. Nevertheless, since we're more concerned about now, I will touch on this amendment only briefly.

Even though the 2nd Amendment is a byproduct of one of the most memorable events in early American history (Massachusetts legislature refused to quarter troops which lead to the Boston Massacre), it does have bearing today. The amendment alludes to a citizen's right to privacy. The Supreme Court has used the right to privacy principle inspired by the 3rd Amendment to protect citizen's right to privacy.

Amendment IV: Search and Seizure. Ratified 12/15/1791.

The right of the people to be secure in their persons, houses, papers, and effects, against unreasonable searches and seizures, shall not be violated, and no Warrants shall issue, but upon probable cause, supported by Oath or affirmation, and particularly describing the place to be searched, and the persons or things to be seized.

This dovetails with the 3rd Amendment in protecting citizen's right to privacy. Before the Constitution, British soldiers often forcefully entered the homes of colonists *without warning* and without *specific cause*. As you can see, adequate warning and specific cause are essential elements in the 4th Amendment.

Today, basically the Supreme Court has said that the police cannot merely come into a citizen's home and sweep for clues to a crime. There has to be, as you've heard, **probable cause**.

Interestingly enough, even though the 4th Amendment states that "the people [are] secure in their persons, houses, papers, and effects" that concept of protection of the "individual" in his or her home now includes wiretapping. However, at the same time, what a person says in the privacy of their own home is available for public consumption and is not protected by the 4th Amendment. Or that which is stated in private and then restated in public is not protected by the 4th Amendment.

At the same time, don't think your garbage which is put on the curb is protected. If you've got something in there it's available to the public, even if it's the police looking for evidence or drugs. No warrant needed in these cases.

Reasonable Searches and Seizures: Here, privacy, as we've seen is a concern, but what of "seizure"? When is it OK to go into someone's home and obtain what is wanted? Probable cause comes into play or the more than sufficient belief that the person in question has committed a crime. However, according to the Supreme Court, there are exceptions in which searches without warrants do not require **probable cause**.

Some of those events are when a police officer on the street believes it necessary to stop and frisk a suspect; or because of 9/11, airport personnel are allowed to search passengers without probable cause; or police are allowed to stop you at a general sobriety checkpoint as long as you're not being singled out, but the same cannot be done for drugs since the program does not have a specific purpose to support highway safety; or the police are allowed a "consent search," such as in your roommate allowing the police in; or drug testing in a place of work; or student searches, such as searching for drugs on campus to keep the campus safe for all students involved.

You get the point.

Finally, we have the warrant clause where the officer involved must go before a civil officer, judge or justice of the peace, who will make a decision if the warrant is justified.

If an officer sees a crime occur and the suspect runs into a home he may make an arrest; however, if a person is a suspect and in his home, a warrant must be obtained.

To search requires probable cause; however, most searches are made without warrants. If you are a suspect you can be searched. If evidence is in plain view, a warrant is not needed. In cases of emergency, a police officer does not need a warrant to enter a home that is burning. Or if a police officer is in hot pursuit, he may follow a suspect into a home or building without a warrant. I'm sure you've seen Cops, yes? Officers can also search cars because they are not as private as a home, and it would be difficult for the officer to obtain a warrant and then re-find the vehicle that may be miles away by the time he does so.

Amendment V: Trial and Punishment, Compensation for Takings. Ratified 12/15/1791.

No person shall be held to answer for a capital, or otherwise infamous crime, unless on a presentment or indictment of a Grand Jury, except in cases arising in the land or naval forces, or in the Militia, when in actual service in time of War or public danger; nor shall any person be subject for the same offense to be twice put in jeopardy of life or limb; nor shall be compelled in any criminal case to be a witness against himself, nor be deprived of life, liberty, or property, without due process of law; nor shall private property be taken for public use, without just compensation.

You've heard about the 5th, yes? As in "I'm taking the fifth." The protection against selfincrimination is the Hollywood right, the star right, but there are four other fifths, as in rights. They all, as per the Constitution in general, limit the power of the government to take action, or more specifically, unjust action against the individual.

First you have the **right to a grand jury**, as opposed to a petit jury, if you are charged of a serious crime. The difference? Grand is 23 jurors; petit is 6 to 12. Petit jury determines fact; Grand jury determines if there is enough evidence to charge a defendant with a crime.

You also have protection against double jeopardy. Basically, this protects against the government from charging, charging, charging the defendant with the crime until it gets a conviction. Considering the resources at hand, this is not too farfetched for the government to do without restraint. However, if there is a mistrial, the accused can be retried or a second trial can occur if there is an appeal or the accused is charged with other crimes.

And the **self-incrimination right** disallows the defendant from testifying against herself.

The Miranda rights allow one to obtain an attorney even if the accused can't' afford one, but more importantly, it protects him from self-incrimination for he has "the right to remain silent." However, if he "give[s] up the right to remain silent, anything [he] say[s] can be used against [him]."

If the accused does speak before these rights are read, what is said will not be allowed in court, unless the police can prove in court that the evidence would eventually have been discovered anyway.

The 5th Amendment also protects "due process of law" or restricts federal government. It basically says that government can't be random in its punishment but must act according to certain laws. There are two categories regarding due process: substantive, the content of a law must be fair, and procedural, the rules by which the law is implemented must be fair.

That clear? Probably not. Let's try that again. A dictionary definition would be, substantive is defining rights and duties as opposed to giving the rules by which rights and duties are established; "substantive law." You've got rights and duties just lying there with their definitions, substantive; to bring them to life, you need give those rules specifics or the procedural.

Need I say more?

The last thing is private property shall not "**be taken for public use, without just compensation.**" Meaning, if the government wants to build a train track through your house or a park in your front yard it has to give you proper incentive. OK, big cash . . . hopefully. But the key point here is that the power of the government to take your property in exchange for some mula is "limited." Not, no they can't! But yes they can, for a fee.

But you know what is not good? Things before the 14th Amendment. Case in point, in Barron v. Baltimore (1833), a wharf owned by Barron was damaged by the city. Barron said pay up; the city said, the Constitution does not apply to states. Barron said, What?!!! Or probably something close to that. But thank heavens for the 14th Amendment, yes? I'm guessing that if you're a gambling man or woman, 14 is your luck number, especially if your last name is Barron *and* you live in the city of Baltimore.

This taking private property for public use, known as **public domain**, is how the government got the highways and railroads built. But now with the 15th Amendment questions are posed as to how much the government can take. The Supreme Court in the past has used zoning laws and historic preservation statues as excuses for regulating property without compensation. Sad but true. However, in the 90s the Court has given more rights to the people, a good thing, yes? However, when the government is justified in taking property, it merely has to pay **fair market value** and not pay for moving or other extraneous costs. Sad, but true.

Personally, I know of a case where a friend of mine who owned a flower store had the connecting wall of her shop taken down by city construction. The city took to replacing the wall but got caught up in so many delays that she finally just sold her business and moved out. She said that the noise and dust was beyond bearable. And guess what? The city wanted the entire building but couldn't get her to move by conventional means so . . . Yes, they had just successfully played the we'll-get-right-back-to-it delay game. Now she's working as a secretary for an English department at a community college, which she says she enjoys for the lack of aggravation it brings . . . for now. So you do have to watch out for big government, but at the same time it is there to protect citizens, if you can get the proper amendments approved and interpreted to your advantage, adequate public awareness going, and proper level of Court consciousness raised. Good luck.

Amendment VI: Right to Speedy Trial, Confrontation of Witnesses. Ratified 12/15/1791.

This amendment was added to actually protect the rights of criminal defendants for a fair trial. Article III's guarantee to a trial in criminal cases is here, but there's also the right to subpoena witnesses and to have a lawyer. This amendment is an attempt, once again, to protect the relatively powerless individual from the greatly powerful state.

In all criminal prosecutions, the accused shall enjoy the right to a speedy and public trial, by an <u>impartial</u> **jury of the State and district wherein the crime shall have been committed, which district shall have been previously ascertained by law, and to be informed of the nature and cause of the accusation; to be confronted with the witnesses against him; to have compulsory process for obtaining witnesses in his favor, and to have the Assistance of Counsel for his** <u>defence</u> **.**

Now the wording states **criminal prosecutions.** What of lesser crimes? If I get caught for going 10 miles an hour over the speed limit, do I get all the above rights? Unfortunately, no.

However, according to this clause, the defendant is promised a speedy trial. But what have you heard of getting trials to court and the "speed" in doing so? Well, unfortunately, there are exceptions. You've heard of the delays, and, yes, if you look at the detail of law code there certainly are exceptions. And that's what we love about law, isn't it? Here you go, check this out. According to U.S. Code: Title 18, Chapter 208, 3161. Time limits and exclusions, section (h):

(h) **The following periods of delay shall be excluded in computing the time within which an information or an indictment must be filed, or in computing the time within which the trial of any such offense must commence:**

(1) Any period of delay resulting from other proceedings concerning the defendant, including but not limited to-

(A) delay resulting from any proceeding, including any examinations, to determine the mental competency or physical capacity of the defendant [*you've seen the movies, this could take years*];

(B) delay resulting from any proceeding, including any examination of the defendant, pursuant to section 2902 [1] of title 28 , United States Code;

(C) delay resulting from deferral of prosecution pursuant to section 2902

Amendment VII: Trial by Jury in Civil Cases. Ratified 12/15/1791.

In Suits at common law, where the value in controversy shall exceed twenty dollars, the right of trial by jury shall be preserved, and no fact tried by a jury, shall be otherwise re-examined in any Court of the United States, than according to the rules of the common law.

OK, you've got criminal cases, cases in which government punishes individuals for committing crimes--Amendment VI--and you've got civil cases, lawsuits between private parties over noncriminal cases such as personal injury and contracts. Here in Amendment VII, the judge's power is limited in throwing out a jury's decision.

As a point of note, to understand a greater portion of the Constitution's effectiveness it comes down to one word and one word only: limit. What the Constitution is attempting to do is limit governmental power because, remember, the colonists were coming from a position of powerlessness being ruled by a despot, King George III.

Now, a trial by jury was ideally written into the Constitution to get "the people" directly involved in government. Ideally, this is a nice idea. Practically, there are problems. Number one is the fact that law over the years has become more and more complex and a civil jury may even inhibit due process of law, according to some experts. Others, as stated above, believe that it's essential that in a democracy--of the people, by the people, for the people to a limited degree--that the public should participate. However, sometimes or most of the time, actually, the public doesn't want to participate.

Case in point, my most popular article of all time of all the hundreds of articles I've written on one of the most popular article directories on the Internet is titled "How to Avoid Jury Duty." Yes, my friends, YOU DON'T WANT JURY DUTY. The reports are conclusive. Apparently, more people want to know more ways to get out of jury duty than anything else I have to offer.

The lengths that people will go to avoid jury duty is considerable. I have one friend who has simply ignored numerous jury summonses. He just throws them in the trash. Something I don't suggest you do. Failure to respond to a jury summons or attend jury duty can result in fines, suspension of driver's license, or in some cases criminal charges. Don't push your luck.

However, I've been summoned three times and attended once. I was excused for financial hardship (I was a student at the time), I was on call for a week but not asked to come in, and then I was on call and asked to come in for jury selection. During jury selection, the majority of people will do a lot of dancing to get out of serving. Of the thirty-plus people I watched take a seat for questioning by the attorneys about half asked the judge for a sidebar. They wanted to talk in private so they could get out of serving. The majority of people had or maybe even invented some type of excuse.

So "ideally" in this greatest of free countries citizens desire to do their duty as a free citizen and serve as a juror. Ideally. Keep in mind that today, American's have been free for quite some time, hundreds of years, and a burning desire to serve one's country by being a juror or to participate in government is nothing new or desirable to a people who have become over the years quite spoiled in their freedom. Americans haven't had a dictator breathing down their necks telling them what to do for a long time. And today, instead of fearing a dictator most Americans fear little, relatively speaking, and have instead become spoiled in the extreme by being able to make their own choices, thus the belief that jury duty is more of an imposition to their free time than a blessing in expressing government-given freedoms.

In Suits at common law, where the value in controversy shall exceed twenty dollars, the right of trial by jury shall be preserved . . .

OK, the amount "in controversy" is no longer "twenty dollars." Now, I think it's twenty-five and some change. Seriously, this dollar amount certainly speaks to a lack of vision by the framers, this point lending itself to the fact that not only were the framers fallible but that Constitutional amendments are essential.

Nevertheless, the point being here that "the right of trial by jury shall be preserved." The right to trial by jury then was essential for a people who were not guaranteed such at the time. And it was certainly better than trial by ordeal, which was used in the Middle Ages, in which one had to do something like hold hot metal to prove he or she was telling the truth; or maybe you were put to battle and you had to win to prove innocence; or how about a trial by oath in which you had to get the greater number of people to swear to God on your behalf than those who did so for your accuser. Now these methods would certainly improve your "speed to trial" right, and if still used today to some degree, maybe as an alternative if you've avoided jury duty, I do believe we would see more enthusiasm for serving as a juror. Just an idea.

Now keep in mind that juries may be competent or incompetent, especially in complex cases that entail evidence, witnesses, delays, etc. But also keep in mind that some scholars say that judges can be incompetent as well. And if you've ever run into highly trained specialists such as physicians and accountants who are incompetent, you know that regardless of the length of alphabet soup after one's name people are people and prone to mistake, bad judgement or just plain negligence.

. . . and no fact tried by a jury, shall be otherwise re-examined in any Court of the United States, than according to the rules of the common law.

Basically, the judge cannot ignore a jury's verdict or tell it what to do, as had been done by British judges in the past. The judge informs the jury of law and the jury deliberates based on this understanding along with the evidence presented. If the jury finds certain facts to be true, the judge, as legal adviser, informs the jury what the verdict will be.

Amendment VIII: Cruel and Unusual Punishment. Ratified 12/15/1791.

Excessive bail shall not be required, nor excessive fines imposed, nor cruel and unusual punishments inflicted.

The 8th Amendment protects prisoners before trial and after conviction, however, protections that may appear limited in regards to a lengthy conviction or death sentence. Here you're not necessarily given an unconditional right to bail but more so that bail when allowed will not be "excessive." Bail is there to make sure the defendant appears in court for his or her trial and any dollar amount above and beyond that necessary amount is not excessive. However, the Bail Reform Act of 1984 disallows bail for excessively dangerous defendants.

And regarding specifically what "cruel and unusual punishment" concerns that's up for debate. It often refers to the extreme or death penalty, for what could be crueler than sentencing one to death unjustly. However, the death penalty is a loaded gun. The death penalty, according to Justice Antonin Scalia, is not unconstitutional, for it is referred to in the 15th Amendment. However, some say that we have progressed as a society to the point where the death penalty should be done away with. Some attest to the one hundred death row inmates who have been released since 1973, and even though these alleged innocent have found freedom, what of those who've been convicted and are actually innocent through found evidence after being put to death? Some even say that evidence may never be found that would acquit a convict sentenced to death, one who many would say for all intents and purposes is innocent. Opponents say, what then?

In another area, according to the Court, the death penalty has been found unconstitutional when applied to juveniles under sixteen or the mentally retarded. But skepticism in regards to one's life should always be abundant, according to George Will: "Capital punishment . . . is a government program, so skepticism is in order."

Amendment IX: Construction of Constitution. Ratified 12/15/1791.

The enumeration in the Constitution, of certain rights, shall not be construed to deny or disparage others retained by the people.

According to Mr. Constitution, James Madison, the 9th Amendment was added to make sure that no one believed that the rights of citizens are restricted to The Bill of Rights. However, the Supreme Court has never used the 9th Amendment in making decisions regarding unremunerated rights. Instead, the Court has used the other amendments in regards to unspoken or unwritten writes.

However, some say the biggest problem with the 9th Amendment is who's doing the protecting? The federal or state courts or the people? There has been much debate regarding the 9th Amendment by judges, scholars, and others; however, as of yet, the Supreme Court has pretty much left it alone. Therefore, this is why it's known as the forgotten amendment.

What is a right, where does it come from, and can it be protected?

Rights come by law, nature, and tradition. Natural laws are innate to humans but aren't necessarily protected by the government. Legal rights are created by the government and may be protected depending on whether that protection comes from the federal or state government or both. However, these created laws or rights can be taken away by the government since it created them. The 9th Amendment says that just because the law or right doesn't exist doesn't mean that it can't. But what right is it talking about? Legal rights or natural rights? And therefore, you can see why this amendments doesn't get much attention.

Amendment X: Powers of the States and People. Ratified 12/15/1791.

The powers not delegated to the United States by the Constitution, nor prohibited by it to the States, are reserved to the States respectively, or to the people.

Here we're talking state power not individual rights like the previous eight amendments.

Through the Constitution, states gave up a lot of rights but get some back with the 10th Amendment. Power between the states and federal government is an ongoing issue, even today, and early on resulted in the Civil War. As the years have passed, the Court has given more and more power to the states, as the 10th Amendment suggests. To show the initial importance of state over federal power, Thomas Jefferson and James Madison believed that to keep the federal under wraps the states could declare acts of Congress unconstitutional.

Numerous southern states did secede causing the Civil War, but even with the south still not over the loss of the war, the federal government interceded on three important occasions in bringing minorities their rights: Brown v. Board of Education (1954), public schools must be segregated; the "Little Rock Nine" (1957) and Eisenhowers protecting the first black students to attend Central High School in Little Rock, Arkansas; and the J. F. K. assigned federal troop protection of black students attending the University of Mississippi (1962). That war or civil war did not break out again is a testament to a burgeoning society, one that was growing in its wisdom and restraint; maybe with divine providence at the backs of the majority attempting to grow with a greater and greater desire to work toward the ideal that all men are created equal.

The People's U.S. Constitution: Amendment XI: Judicial Limits. Ratified 2/7/1795.

The Judicial power of the United States shall not be construed to extend to any suit in law or equity, commenced or prosecuted against one of the United States by Citizens of another State, or by Citizens or Subjects of any Foreign State.

OK, this amendment is supposed to protect states against lawsuits, but does it? Yes and no. It's just like Constitutional law to provide such a dichotomy, isn't it? So what's up? Well, here we go again.

Many a state was fretting that Article III would leave them open to lawsuits, so the Eleventh Amendment was born. Even though the federal told the states not to worry because they had sovereign immunity (a state or nation not to be sued without consent) along came Chisholm v. Georgia (1793) in which the Court OK'd the request for Georgia to pay a Revolutionary War debt. What was the Court's excuse? You guessed it, that sovereignty only applied to the federal government.

So even though some of the framers and the Court often told the people not to worry about rights and amendments regarding the protecting of those rights ("Oh, it's OK, Mr. And Mrs. Citizen, we've got your collective back" Framers and Court et. al.), it becomes more and more clear why so many citizens were screaming and clamoring for the specific protection of their rights. But of course, we don't have to worry about protecting our rights today, do we? For we all know that Big Brother has our best intentions in mind at all times, right? Right.

OK, so how much does the 11th Amendment actually protect states' rights?

Number one, it doesn't protect states from being sued by the U.S. government in a federal court, so get that out of your heads, states. And the Court has also decided that the 14th and 15th Amendments allow it to hold states accountable for violating certain rights. But then again . . . The Court, in recent years, has *not* allowed citizens to sue states for patent infringement, age discrimination, and violation of fair labor standards. So now we go back to prioritization of rights: state vs. individual. What gives? Well, because we've gotten so big as a country, it's actually becoming more and more difficult for the federal government to bring lawsuits on the behalf of citizens. Consider that if during a particular session the Supreme Court is hearing cases regarding such things as the right to bear arms, the death penalty for child rape, and Guantanamo Bay prisoner rights, hearing about your case on age discrimination probably won't happen. Maybe if the number of justices was increased tenfold individual citizens would get their just dessert. But what do I know, I'm just Joe Average citizen. Not my call.

And this all leads to the ideal Constitution and the practical Constitution and the separation of fact and fiction. There's the fiction of what is ideal but the fact of the imperfection of applying that ideal with fallible, agenda-laden individuals to a changing, shifting world.

Enough said.

The People's U.S. Constitution: Amendment XII: Choosing the President, Vice-President. Ratified 6/15/1804.

The Electors shall meet in their respective states, and vote by ballot for President and VicePresident, one of whom, at least, shall not be an inhabitant of the same state with themselves; they shall name in their ballots the person voted for as President, and in distinct ballots the person voted for as Vice-President, and they shall make distinct lists of all persons voted for as President, and of all persons voted for as Vice-President and of the number of votes for each, which lists they shall sign and certify, and transmit sealed to the seat of the government of the United States, directed to the President of the Senate;

The President of the Senate shall, in the presence of the Senate and House of Representatives, open all the certificates and the votes shall then be counted;

The person having the greatest Number of votes for President, shall be the President, if such number be a majority of the whole number of Electors appointed; and if no person have such majority, then from the persons having the highest numbers not exceeding three on the list of those voted for as President, the House of Representatives shall choose immediately, by ballot, the President. But in choosing the President, the votes shall be taken by states, the representation from each state having one vote; a quorum for this purpose shall consist of a member or members from two-thirds of the states, and a majority of all the states shall be necessary to a choice. And if the House of Representatives shall not choose a President whenever the right of choice shall devolve upon them, before the fourth day of March next following, then the Vice-President shall act as President, as in the case of the death or other constitutional disability of the President.

The person having the greatest number of votes as Vice-President, shall be the VicePresident, if such number be a majority of the whole number of Electors appointed, and if no person have a majority, then from the two highest numbers on the list, the Senate shall choose the Vice-President; a <u>quorum</u> for the purpose shall consist of two-thirds of the whole number of Senators, and a majority of the whole number shall be necessary to a choice. But no person constitutionally ineligible to the office of President shall be eligible to that of VicePresident of the United States.

Got all that? There's a lot here but we're not going to spend a lot of time discussing.

It's pretty simple. This amendment says that the president and vice president will be elected on separate ballots as opposed to the single ballot suggested under Article II. Or stated in another way, the electors vote for a President and for a Vice President rather than two choices for President and he or she who comes in second gets the VP.

But why? Well, so that the top two people won't be from opposing parties and end up being Pres. and VP like that which happened in 1796 to Jefferson (Democratic-Republican) and Adams (Federalist).

Just imagine today something like an Obama / McCain presidency. Would either want to be VP to the other? I think not. They may put on political airs and confess to the workability of their plight to David

Letterman and Jay Leno and the general public, but it would certainly be far from the truth.

Or how about this scenario? McCain and Palin tie and Palin doesn't withdraw from the race allowing McCain to take the presidency, so the House of Representatives vote and Palin becomes president. The problems here are manifold, especially if you're not a true Palin supporter. So how do we fix all this?

Viola! the Twelfth Amendment. Fixed . . . Kind of.

Way back then, some argued that the 12 th Amendment would encourage presidential candidates to seek a person of "moderate talents" for vice president. Those seriously opposed to Palin running would certainly see the wisdom behind this statement.

There's some other stuff in here about the VP counting all the votes before a joint session of Congress. What happens if a president isn't chosen by the beginning of a new term or if no vice presidential candidate has a majority of the votes, and yada, yada, yada.

I guess that if you're interested in this minutia you can go back and read it, or if you're a member of Congress and you need to know the rules; otherwise, me and the rest of the party are moving on.

The People's U.S. Constitution: Amendment XIII: Slavery Abolished. Ratified 12/6/1865.

1. Neither slavery nor involuntary servitude, except as a punishment for crime whereof the party shall have been duly convicted, shall exist within the United States, or any place subject to their jurisdiction .

2. Congress shall have power to enforce this article by appropriate legislation.

This is certainly not a living amendment or one that is referred to, to make current law. However, it is one of the most important, for it begins in earnest to uphold the ideal for the persecuted, for the minority that "All men are created equal, that they are endowed by their Creator with certain unalienable rights that among these are life, liberty, and the pursuit of happiness."

This was certainly a controversial topic, so much so that the framers said it couldn't be touched until 1808 or sometime after the ratification of the Constitution so this new country could at least get up on its feet before it took this issue head on.

As a side note, when one thinks of the freeing of the slaves, Lincoln's image comes to mind. However, it would be false to think that Lincoln was not prejudice or that his Emancipation Proclamation was enacted only to free the slaves, for he was a politician, after all.

Lincoln was like most in the U.S. at the time, a racist. How could he not be? It was the prevalent mindset of the time. Just as today one would be hard pressed not to see overt expression of the inferiority of a particular race as wrong and politically incorrect. Yet one day while on a riverboat, Lincoln saw a slave shackled to the boat, and it had a profound effect on his sense of the slave's humanity.

But Lincoln did try to keep the states together by supporting the Corwin Amendment which if ratified would *not* allow Congress to outlaw slavery. Even his Emancipation Proclamation of 1863 was more of a war-ending impetus package than a kind gesture to slaves, for even though it did free slaves in the South-something no member of the Southern Confederate States would ever agree to do-it planted the idea of freedom more solidly in the minds of the slaves (a disruptive notion) and the North's intentions in the minds of the whites.

The People's U.S. Constitution: Amendment XIV: Citizenship Rights or Equal Protection of the Laws. Ratified 7/9/1868.

1. All persons born or naturalized in the United States, and subject to the jurisdiction thereof, are citizens of the United States and of the State wherein they reside. No State shall make or enforce any law which shall abridge the privileges or immunities of citizens of the United States; nor shall any State deprive any person of life, liberty, or property, without due process of law; nor deny to any person within its jurisdiction the equal protection of the laws.

2. Representatives shall be apportioned among the several States according to their respective numbers, counting the whole number of persons in each State, excluding Indians not taxed. But when the right to vote at any election for the choice of electors for President and Vice-President of the United States, Representatives in Congress, the Executive and Judicial officers of a State, or the members of the Legislature thereof, is denied to any of the male inhabitants of such State, being twenty-one years of age, and citizens of the United States, or in any way abridged, except for participation in rebellion, or other crime, the basis of representation therein shall be reduced in the proportion which the number of such male citizens shall bear to the whole number of male citizens twenty-one years of age in such State.

3. No person shall be a Senator or Representative in Congress, or elector of President and Vice-President, or hold any office, civil or military, under the United States, or under any State, who, having previously taken an oath, as a member of Congress, or as an officer

of the United States, or as a member of any State legislature, or as an executive or judicial officer of any State, to support the Constitution of the United States, shall have engaged in insurrection or rebellion against the same, or given aid or comfort to the enemies thereof. But Congress may by a vote of two-thirds of each House, remove such disability.

4. The validity of the public debt of the United States, authorized by law, including debts incurred for payment of pensions and bounties for services in suppressing insurrection or rebellion, shall not be questioned. But neither the United States nor any State shall assume or pay any debt or obligation incurred in aid of insurrection or rebellion against the United States, or any claim for the loss or emancipation of any slave; but all such debts, obligations and claims shall be held illegal and void.

5. The Congress shall have power to enforce, by appropriate legislation, the provisions of this article.

Because of its importance, the 14th Amendment has been referred to as the New Constitution, but what makes this one greater than all the rest? It is the amendment that the Court used to apply the provisions of the Bill of Rights to the states. Remember how often the phrase "doesn't apply to the states" has been used by the Court in past amendments? It's an interesting point to bring up, because how many Joe and Jane average citizens believe (or never thought about) the Constitution applies to citizens at the state level? Of course, the definition of federal is *a union of states that recognizes the sovereignty of a central authority or government while retaining certain* **residual** *powers of government.*

But in using your thesaurus if you click on "residual", one of the words that appears is "leftover." Who wants a whole bunch of leftovers? So therein is the importance of the 14th Amendment. If it wasn't for this amendment, we'd still be eating leftovers a greater portion of the time. Nothing like a cold slice of pizza for breakfast or a turkey sandwich the day after Thanksgiving, but a steady diet of leftovers is seldom healthy or preferred.

The 14th Amendment also attempts to make up for the lack of political rights received by former slaves and to negate the Black Codes or a "separate but equal" status, for even though they were physically freed through the Emancipation Proclamation, blacks did not begin to fully receive their rights until after the Civil Rights Act of 1964. And even though the 14th Amendment, which was ratified in 1868, sought "equal protection" for all citizens, we all know that the receiving of those rights even to this day is a work in progress.

1. All persons born or naturalized in the United States, and subject to the jurisdiction thereof, are citizens of the United States and of the State wherein they reside. No State shall make or enforce any law which shall abridge the privileges or immunities of citizens of the United States; nor shall any State deprive any person of life, liberty, or property, without due process of law; nor deny to any person within its jurisdiction the equal protection of the laws.

It used to be left up to the states to determine citizenship. Now citizenship is a national designation. Here, for the first time, regardless of race, color, creed, "all persons born or naturalized in the United States" are citizens of those states. All states, including the one he or she is born in.

And in order for southern states to be added back to the union after the Civil War, they were *required* to ratify the 14th Amendment, the cornerstone of the government's plan for Reconstruction.

Some Supreme Court justices have believed that the Bill of Rights should be selectively applied to the states or what is called "selective incorporation." Others believed that this gave the Court too much power and subjective reign over decisions, therefore, the "total incorporation" philosophy or applying all the provisions of the Bill of Rights to the states.

Which has won out? Selective incorporation, for the following rights in the first eight amendments have not been applied to the states: the right to keep and bear arms (2nd Amendment) even though this has changed somewhat in recent years (see my comments in The People's U.S. Constitution: Amendments II-IV); the restriction on quartering troops (3rd Amendment); trial by jury in civil cases (7th Amendment); and the ban on excessive bail and fines (Eight Amendment). And we're not concerned about the 9th and 10th Amendments because they don't apply to the states. They may mention "the people" and "states" but they do not *directly* protect individual rights.

The "due process of law" clause of the 14th Amendment is a protection of what the Court calls enumerated rights or rights that are not specifically in the Constitution. I hope you can see by this statement the inherent problems of "due process." For since nothing is specifically stated, who states? Well, whoever happens to be a Supreme Court justice, that's who. And depending on the subjective nature of your call as Supreme Court justice, "due process" protection may or may not protect.

For example, what if you as a justice believe in laissez faire or government not stepping in to regulate business? In this case, you potentially give more power to the companies. If you oppose laissez faire philosophy, you give more power to the people. Which is it? And what's the good of all this "due process"? Once again, it comes down to the whim of the Court. But keep in mind that since this is the United States--a government of the people, by the people, for the people, allegedly--in order to keep the people happy, you may decide to alter your opinion if the majority speaking loudly in your ear opposes your interpretation of the protection of enumerated rights. I know judges are elected to life-terms but, hey, judges are people too, most anyway.

U.S. citizens may complain and fret and worry and rail against "the system," but what's the option? Federalism may not be the ideal, and it sure isn't as neat and easy as Communism where as a citizen you simply follow along or get thrown in jail or strung up for disobedience. But you do have a choice, even though a choice to leave these good states may end in fewer choices, but again, your choice.

But here's a little despotism in your federalism to give you a taste of our government's imperfection and, may I say, its imbecility.

In Buck vs. Bell (1927) Carrie Buck was to be sterilized for being an "imbecile." At the time, there was a belief that the human race could be purified through eugenics-selective breeding to improve the human race. Those who were selected were not necessarily unintelligent but poor. Justice Oliver Wendell Holmes allowed Buck's sterilization because "Three generation of imbeciles is enough."

But who's the imbecile here? You can plainly see why the subjectivity of the Constitution's interpretation and the leaving of the "greater" decisions in the hands of the unelected and life-serving few is problematic for many American citizens. But get these guys in office, if you will, with the vote, let them stay, say, three or four years, and they have to work to get reelected, I'm sure we'll see a difference in the overall decision-making of the Court.

And I'm really not sure why justices aren't elected and take office for life. Maybe it was done early on because being a judge was not seen as a great job and to keep people they were given life sentences (the double meaning here should be noted) or a promise of steady employment. In the early goings of this country, many took a judgeship because of "last resort" tactics. But it appears to me that a change in the election of our Supreme Court judges is certainly needed.

Now let's consider the Equal Protection Clause. A biggie, for this is the first time we see the word "equal" specifically expressed in the Constitution. The intention here is to avoid discrimination and it restricts the states. Yes, I said "states." So maybe this federalism isn't so reciprocating as we the people believe were lead to believe.

But this amendment is a biggie, as I so gracefully stated above, because its main purpose is to protect minorities from racial discrimination. And it should, for in the past the Court allowed racial segregation of public facilities, the Japanese during WWII to be interned, and The Chinese

Exclusion Act (the only time an entire race was specifically excluded by the government).

This is not ancient history, for professor James W. Loewen states in *Sundown Towns: A Hidden Dimension of American Racism* that "Towns such as Anna and Jonesboro are often called sundown towns,' owing to the signs that many of them formerly sported at their corporate limits-signs that usually said 'Nigger, Don't Let the Sun Go Down on You in __.' Anna-Jonesboro had such signs on Highway 127 as recently as the 1970s." Thirty years is but a spit in the bucket of recorded history. You can now stop wondering why such an insidious disease like racism is believed by many to be alive and well, for a disease that has lasted thousands of years is not simply eradicated in a few decades by a few words in a document.

Once again, I say "due process" and the protection of "enumerated rights"? But whose rights? In Plessy v. Ferguson, a case that involved racial segregation in public places, Homer Plessy believed that Jim Crow Laws reinforced a "badge of inferiority." The court thought otherwise: "If this be so, it is not by reason of anything found in the act, but solely because the colored race chooses to put that construction upon it." Ah, the wisdom of our illustrious courts.

And if you think that all citizens of these United States have been protected by our most important document, the Law of the Land, one must ponder its lack of ability to do so, especially considering the 4,700 people who were lynched between 1882 and 1944. Unfortunately, for many the Law of the Land has stood more for the modern day shorthand LOL.

But even women were discriminated against by the Court. Justice Joseph P. Bradley said that being a wife and mother, according to God, is "the paramount destiny and mission of women." And even as late as the early 1900s the Court believed that women should work limited hours on the grounds that they are "the weaker sex." Also, women shouldn't work in bars because of the morality issue-women are naturally more susceptible to being harmed by immoral environments. Or women being exempt from jury duty because they "need to be at home with their families."

Need I say more about "enumeration" and "due process" and their limitations as a result of human error and bias? Even the bias of our unelected "smart" people?

But women still are getting the short end of the stick. According to the Court, sex is not a suspect class, as much as race is. The Court uses a less demanding test than "compelling interest" for classification based on gender. The Equal Rights Amendment stated that "Equality of rights under the law shall not be denied or abridged by the United States nor by any state on account of sex." Yet the amendment was never ratified.

So far we've been speaking mostly about citizens; however, the Equal Protection Clause also applies to aliens. Regarding benefits, Congress has complete control of immigration and who gets what. The States, however, since the Court has sovereignty here, can't deny even illegal immigrants certain benefits such as education.

2. Representatives shall be <u>apportioned</u> among the several States according to their respective numbers, counting the whole number of persons in each State, excluding Indians not taxed. . . .

The 13th Amendment may have abolished slavery, but it said nothing about fixing the provision in Article I, Section 2, or the statement that slaves shall count as three-fifths of a person regarding representation.

. . . But when the right to vote at any election for the choice of electors for President and Vice-President of the United States, Representatives in Congress, the Executive and Judicial officers of a State, or the members of the Legislature thereof, is denied to any of the *male inhabitants* of such State, being twenty-one years of age, and citizens of the United States, . . .

Here we see the all-too-troublesome word "male." At the time it was written, what did that mean? Eventually, it meant more work, actually, for there would have to be separate amendments for not only women, but black men (for "male," even though it was not specifically stated, meant "white male inhabitants"), and eventually, eighteen-year-olds on up.

. . . or in any way abridged, except for participation in rebellion, or other crime, the basis of representation therein shall be reduced in the proportion which the number of such male citizens shall bear to the whole number of male citizens twenty-one years of age in such State.

This provision punishes states for not allowing African American's to vote; however, it says nothing of the states having to stop such practices. Odd, yet a technicality nevertheless.

3. No person shall be a Senator or Representative in Congress, or elector of President and Vice-President, or hold any office, civil or military, under the United States, or under any

State, who, having previously taken an oath, as a member of Congress, or as an officer of the United States, or as a member of any State legislature, or as an executive or judicial officer of any State, to support the Constitution of the United States, shall have engaged in insurrection or rebellion against the same, or given aid or comfort to the enemies thereof. But Congress may by a vote of two-thirds of each House, remove such disability.

This is post-Civil War stuff. Basically, you couldn't hold federal or state office if you supported the Confederacy.

Let's move on.

4. The validity of the public debt of the United States, authorized by law, including debts incurred for payment of pensions and bounties for services in suppressing insurrection or rebellion, shall not be questioned. But neither the United States nor any State shall assume or pay any debt or obligation incurred in aid of insurrection or rebellion against the United States, or any claim for the loss or emancipation of any slave; but all such debts, obligations and claims shall be held illegal and void.

What's this? This recognizes and validates Union debt from the Civil War. However, it makes it evident that federal or state government will not take on any of the debt.

5. The Congress shall have power to enforce, by appropriate legislation, the provisions of this article.

Here is simply a statement of the federal government's power to give Congress the authority to pass legislation to enforce its provisions.

The People's U.S. Constitution: Amendment XVI: Status of Income Tax Clarified. Ratified 2/3/1913.

The Congress shall have power to lay and collect taxes on incomes, from whatever source derived, without apportionment among the several States, and without regard to any census or enumeration.

OK, this one's a popular amendment with the citizens, near and dear to our hearts, for who doesn't love knowing all about taxes and especially paying them?

Great! Let's get into it.

This amendment came about because of the Progressive Era in the 1900s and a desire by the government to get more revenue or its hands deeper into our collective pockets. Great stuff, huh? Oh, I know you're enjoying this. Anyway . . .

Unfortunately for us, the 16th Amendment made income taxes Constitutional when applied to individuals but "without apportionment among the . . . States."

This amendment has created serious stomach acid build up for me.

Let's move on.

The People's U.S. Constitution: Amendment XVII - Senators Elected by Popular Vote. Ratified 4/8/1913.

The Senate of the United States shall be composed of two Senators from each State, elected by the people thereof, for six years; and each Senator shall have one vote. The electors in each State shall have the qualifications requisite for electors of the most numerous branch of the State legislatures.

When vacancies happen in the representation of any State in the Senate, the executive authority of such State shall issue writs of election to fill such vacancies: Provided, That the legislature of any State may empower the executive thereof to make temporary appointments until the people fill the vacancies by election as the legislature may direct.

This amendment shall not be so construed as to affect the election or term of any Senator chosen before it becomes valid as part of the Constitution.

Here's another amendment inspired by the Progressive Era. Here the people can now vote for senators rather than leave it up to legislators who get weak in the knees when they see large sums of money coming their way from corporations advocating certain senators who, I'm just guessing here, will do a lot of nice things for them, things like, oh, deregulation and things like that.

So many were happy about this amendment, not least of all the people, for now not only could they limit the corruption in the Senate, but they could stretch their legs by going out for a nice walk to the poles.

But I think you may see a problem with this amendment. Yes, it was the senators who were getting corrupted by the corrupt. OK, they were corrupt too, but you know what I mean. So passing this with a two-thirds vote by the offenders was not a given. However, the pump had already been greased, for most states had required state legislators through provisions to consider being voted in by the people.

And on we go.

The People's U.S. Constitution: Amendment XVIII: Liquor Abolished. Ratified 1/16/1919. Repealed by Amendment 21, 12/5/1933.

1.   After one year from the ratification of this article the manufacture, sale, or transportation of intoxicating liquors within, the importation thereof into, or the exportation thereof from the United States and all territory subject to the jurisdiction thereof for beverage purposes is hereby prohibited.

2.   The Congress and the several States shall have concurrent power to enforce this article by appropriate legislation.

3.   This article shall be inoperative unless it shall have been ratified as an amendment to the Constitution by the legislatures of the several States, as provided in the Constitution, within seven years from the date of the submission hereof to the States by the Congress.

This one came about most likely because of the Progressive Era or the let's-change-society-for-the-better-through-the-Constitution philosophy or this-document-may-just-be-the-place-to-fix-those-things-called-humans. Delusional thinking, of course.

Sounds like an experiment, right? Well, it was still relatively early in our history and people were a bit naïve. This can be borne out by the fact that people thought that the Constitution could even outlaw crime, poverty, and broken homes.

Here's how one American saw alcohol and its environment: "The salon is the sum of all villainies. It is worse than war or pestilence. It is the parent of all crimes and the mother of all sins." Billy Sunday

The problem with the amendment was that it forced the making and drinking of alcohol underground into speakeasies run by mobs. The unworkable nature of the amendment lead to the 21st Amendment that repealed it.

Amendment XIX: Women's Suffrage. Ratified 8/18/1920.

The right of citizens of the United States to vote shall not be denied or abridged by the United States or by any State on account of sex.

Congress shall have power to enforce this article by appropriate legislation.

Here's one for the ladies . . . finally.

Did you know that woman's suffrage began in the 1790s? Yes, Mary Wollstonecraft wrote *A Vindication of the Rights of Women*. She was known as the first feminist. But even before Wollstonecraft was Abigail Adams who told her famous husband and the others of the Continental Congress in a letter dated March, 1776 to "...remember the ladies, and be more generous and favorable to them than your ancestors. Do not put such unlimited power into the hands of the Husbands. Remember all Men would be tyrants if they could. If particular care and attention is not paid to the Ladies we are determined to foment a Rebellion, and will not hold ourselves bound by any Laws in which we have no voice, or Representation."

That revolution came in earnest through the organized suffragette movement established by Susan B. Anthony and Elizabeth Cady Stanton in 1848.

The more than hundred-twenty years it took for woman to get the vote testifies to the fact that change is not easy or fast when overcoming hundreds if not thousands of years of poor, incomplete and inaccurate thinking.

The People's U.S. Constitution: Amendment XX: Presidential, Congressional Terms or Lame Ducks. Ratified 1/23/1933.

1.   The terms of the President and Vice President shall end at noon on the 20th day of January, and the terms of Senators and Representatives at noon on the 3d day of January, of the years in which such terms would have ended if this article had not been ratified; and the terms of their successors shall then begin.

2.   The Congress shall assemble at least once in every year, and such meeting shall begin at noon on the 3d day of January, unless they shall by law appoint a different day.

3.   If, at the time fixed for the beginning of the term of the President, the President elect shall have died, the Vice President elect shall become President. If a President shall not have been chosen before the time fixed for the beginning of his term, or if the President elect shall have failed to qualify, then the Vice President elect shall act as President until a President shall have qualified; and the Congress may by law provide for the case wherein neither a President elect nor a Vice President elect shall have qualified, declaring who shall then act as President, or the manner in which one who is to act shall be selected, and such person shall act accordingly until a President or Vice President shall have qualified.

4.   The Congress may by law provide for the case of the death of any of the persons from whom the House of Representatives may choose a President whenever the right of choice shall have devolved upon them, and for the case of the death of any of the persons from

whom the Senate may choose a Vice President whenever the right of choice shall have devolved upon them.

5.   Sections 1 and 2 shall take effect on the 15th day of October following the ratification of this article.

6.   This article shall be inoperative unless it shall have been ratified as an amendment to the Constitution by the legislatures of three-fourths of the several States within seven years from the date of its submission.

Section 1:

This one limits the amount of time lame ducks can be in office. I guess 7-11 parking lots are not the only place loitering is frowned upon.

As many are aware, the presidential inauguration takes place January 20th. It used to be in March. Way too much loitering for most, thus the 20th Amendment.

But you'll notice that in section 1 that Senators and Representatives get the boot early, January 3rd. This is so the new Congress will have time, if needed, to choose a president before January 20th.

Section 2:

This section got rid of the four-month delay (Congress began in December while the inauguration took place in January) that initially existed because back then they didn't have planes, trains, and automobiles or phones, faxes, and the Internet. It took a while to get around and to get in touch.

Section 3:

What if the president-elect should die? Who takes over? The vice president, according to Section 3. If no president is elected when the term begins, you get the VP until one is elected. And then there's the stuff about what happens when there's no president or vice president qualified then Congress picks the pres. and VP.

Section 4:

So what happens if the candidates chosen for president and vice president die between the meeting of the Electoral College in December and the counting of the electoral votes in Congress on Jan. 6? Want to know? Read Section 4.

Section 5:

Need sufficient notice to determine when the old ends and the new begins, Congress? Here's your chance, for Sections 1 and 2 will not be ratified until Oct. 15, so you can have time to clean you lockers or move your stuff in.

Section 6:

Time and method of ratification.

OK, ready for the last seven amendments?

Stay tuned. We're almost done.

The People's U.S. Constitution: Amendment XXI : Amendment 18 Repealed. Ratified 12/5/1933.

1. The eighteenth article of amendment to the Constitution of the United States is hereby repealed.

2. The transportation or importation into any State, Territory, or possession of the United
   States for delivery or use therein of intoxicating liquors, in violation of the laws thereof, is hereby prohibited.

3. The article shall be inoperative unless it shall have been ratified as an amendment to the Constitution by conventions in the several States, as provided in the Constitution, within seven years from the date of the submission hereof to the States by the Congress.

Our first amendment repealed, but a good example of why the Constitution needs to be amendable and un-amendable for improvement. This amendment came on the heels of the death of Prohibition. Maybe a good indicator of the need for separation between church and state. Let the government govern the law and the church govern the soul.

The repeal was also timely for it opened up jobs in breweries and distilleries in a depressive era.

In Section 2, we see only for the second time the Constitution telling citizens that they cannot do something. But in the "not doing" it has set them free, as it did to so many slaves in the 13th Amendment, the only other time citizens were forbidden certain conduct.

The Supreme Court has ruled that Section 2 gives the states authority to regulate alcohol; its consumption not its transportation to other states. The lack of restriction to regulate commerce between states is covered by the Commerce Clause.

Probably the most important result of the repeal was the creation of a new sport called stock car racing. One which came from all the modified cars used in not only getting cargo to destinations on time but also just getting there . . . period, for the police couldn't keep up with these souped-up cars. Maybe this is why stock car racing is the most watched sport on TV. Everyone who's ever had a cop car bearing down on them from behind would love to have a vehicle that could easily put an unrecoverable distance between him and his pursuer. Ka-chow! Ka-ka-ka-chow!

The People's U.S. Constitution: Amendment XXII: Presidential Term Limits. Ratified 2/27/1951.

1. No person shall be elected to the office of the President more than twice, and no person who has held the office of President, or acted as President, for more than two years of a term to which some other person was elected President shall be elected to the office of the President more than once. But this Article shall not apply to any person holding the office of President, when this Article was proposed by the Congress, and shall not prevent any person who may be holding the office of President, or acting as President, during the term within which this Article becomes operative from holding the office of President or acting as President during the remainder of such term.

2. This article shall be inoperative unless it shall have been ratified as an amendment to the Constitution by the legislatures of three-fourths of the several States within seven years from the date of its submission to the States by the Congress.

Did you know that before this amendment Franklin Delano Roosevelt was elected to a fourth term? Not the type of government the framers had envisioned. Few desired to allow a president to roost in the White House, creating the potential for a much despised Monarchial rule so many of the colonists were looking to avoid in this newest of nations.

And for you Republicans, here's a scary proposition: "It's a good thing we've got a 22nd Amendment or I would run again." Bill Clinton

If you look closely at Section 1, you'll see that the maximum number of years a president can actually serve is 10. Yes, 10. Not 8. For if a vice president becomes president and serves no more than two years, he or she can be elected to a maximum of two terms. For you non-math majors that's ten years.

However, because of the two-term limit, a lame-duck situation was created, meaning, since we know the president is out at the end of his second term he loses influence. Not in the case of George W. Bush. He lost all influence long before he got anywhere near the end of his second term. Sorry George. ;=)

The People's U.S. Constitution: Amendment XXIII: Presidential Vote for District of Columbia. Ratified 3/29/1961.

1. The District constituting the seat of Government of the United States shall appoint in such manner as the Congress may direct: A number of electors of President and Vice President equal to the whole number of Senators and Representatives in Congress to which the District would be entitled if it were a State, but in no event more than the least populous State; they shall be in addition to those appointed by the States, but they shall be considered, for the purposes of the election of President and Vice President, to be electors appointed by a State; and they shall meet in the District and perform such duties as provided by the twelfth article of amendment.

2. The Congress shall have power to enforce this article by appropriate legislation.

OK, a little background about our nation's capital, if I please.

The City of Washington was originally a part of the Territory of Columbia until it was combined by An Act of Congress in 1871. Currently, on weekends, the population is about half a million. During the week it swells to about ten times that size with the influx of commuters. This "work area" was defined in 2004 as Washington-Arlington-Alexandria, DC-VA-MD-WV MSA, as defined by the U.S. States Office of Management and Budget (OMB). So if you work in the area, you're well known for telling people that you'll meet them for lunch in

"Washington-ArlingtonAlexandria, DC-VA-MD-WV MSA." That's a mouthful, but really just practice for lunch, isn't it?

Let's move on.

Did you know that the five-hundred-fifty-eight thousand plus citizens of Washington D.C. live in "one of the largest blocs of disenfranchised voters in the world"? (Mayor Anthony Williams).

Yes, they do, for they do not have representation. They do have a non-voting at-large Congressional delegate, but no senators. Well, lots of senators, really, all of them, but none of them represent Washington D.C. And until this 23rd Amendment, people of D.C., or what is commonly known as Washington or the District, couldn't vote for president until 1961, which isn't that long ago historically. To this day, you may have family members or know someone from the area who can tell you more about this.

But why this need for The United States Congress to have supreme authority over the area?

In Federalist No. 43, James Madison states the need for a federal district and a need to be distinct from the states to provide, mostly, for its own safety. Why? Well, in the Pennsylvania Mutiny of 1783, the state of Pennsylvania (where Congress resided at the time) refused to protect Congress from an anti-government protest of some 400 Continental soldiers. Also, it was Madison who had to move out of the White House for repairs after the British burned it down in the War of 1812.

The People's U.S. Constitution: Amendment XXIV : Poll Tax Barred. Ratified 1/23/1964.

1. The right of citizens of the United States to vote in any primary or other election for President or Vice President, for electors for President or Vice President, or for Senator or Representative in Congress, shall not be denied or abridged by the United States or any State by reason of failure to pay any poll tax or other tax.

2. The Congress shall have power to enforce this article by appropriate legislation.

   If you're poor or a minority, you're always a target for discrimination. (See the Florida vote recount of 2000 and the discrimination or lack of attention to Katrina sufferers who were mostly poor and black).

   Previous to the Sixties, there was a lot of discrimination against the poor, even whites (why the Irish were discriminated against for so long). It used to be that you could keep these "undesirables" from voting by requiring voters to own land. However, this limitation was greatly eradicated by the Jacksonian era. So what's a bigot to do? Inflict the poll tax or head tax, a tax that had to be paid in order to vote. Even though it wasn't much, if you were poor, the amount in most cases was prohibitive.

The People's U.S. Constitution: Amendment XXV: Presidential Disability and Succession. Ratified 2/10/1967.

1. In case of the removal of the President from office or of his death or resignation, the Vice President shall become President.

2. Whenever there is a vacancy in the office of the Vice President, the President shall nominate a Vice President who shall take office upon confirmation by a majority vote of both Houses of Congress.

3. Whenever the President transmits to the President pro tempore of the Senate and the Speaker of the House of Representatives his written declaration that he is unable to discharge the powers and duties of his office, and until he transmits to them a written declaration to the contrary, such powers and duties shall be discharged by the Vice President as Acting President.

4. Whenever the Vice President and a majority of either the principal officers of the executive departments or of such other body as Congress may by law provide, transmit to the President pro tempore of the Senate and the Speaker of the House of Representatives their written declaration that the President is unable to discharge the powers and duties of his office, the Vice President shall immediately assume the powers and duties of the office as Acting President.

Thereafter, when the President transmits to the President pro tempore of the Senate and the Speaker of the House of Representatives his written declaration that no inability exists, he shall resume the powers and duties of his office unless the Vice President and a majority of either the principal officers of the executive department or of such

other body as Congress may by law provide, transmit within four days to the President pro tempore of the Senate and the Speaker of the House of Representatives their written declaration that the President is unable to discharge the powers and duties of his office. Thereupon Congress shall decide the issue, assembling within forty eight hours for that purpose if not in session. If the Congress, within twenty one days after receipt of the latter written declaration, or, if Congress is not in session, within twenty one days after Congress is required to assemble, determines by two thirds vote of both Houses that the President is unable to discharge the powers and duties of his office, the Vice President shall continue to discharge the same as
Acting President; otherwise, the President shall resume the powers and duties of his office.

With the assassination of JFK, the question of who should succeed a president who died in office or became temporarily incapacitated came into full consideration. And what of a vice president who encountered similar circumstances?

As we now know, the vice president takes over if the president is removed from office, impeached, or dies or cannot serve in full capacity for whatever reason. In the case of Spiro Agnew, President Nixon had to assign a new vice president after Agnew's conviction of tax evasion. In 1974, with Nixon's resignation, Ford becoming president and nominating Nelson Rockefeller to vice president, the 25th became a much needed amendment.

If the president can't function to his full capacity, he informs the Vice President and Speaker of the House "his written declaration that he is unable to discharge the powers and duties of his office" **(Section 3)**, and the Vice President takes over until told otherwise by the President.

In **Section 4** the president can no longer act for himself; therefore, "the Vice President and a majority of either the principle officers of the executive departments or of such other body as Congress may by law provide" inform the Vice President and Speaker of the House that this is the case and the Vice President takes over. Note here that it's never just one person making these decisions, an allusion to checks and balances. And to continue that theme, Section 4 allows the President to contest a decision of disability made by the Vice President and a majority of the cabinet. Congress must then decide by a two-thirds vote who should be in office.

The People's U.S. Constitution: Amendment XXVI: Voting Age Set to 18 Years. Ratified 7/1/1971.

1. The right of citizens of the United States, who are eighteen years of age or older, to vote shall not be denied or abridged by the United States or by any State on account of age.

2. The Congress shall have power to enforce this article by appropriate legislation.

If you turned eighteen after June of 1971, the 26th Amendment is your favorite; that is if you like voting. Vietnam Vets were stating that if you were old enough to die, you were old enough to vote, thus the 25th Amendment that lowered the voting age from 21 to 18.

During WWII some states allowed those younger than 21 to vote. In the Voting Rights Act of 1970, the voting age was set to 18. However, in Oregon vs. Mitchell (1970) the Supreme Court ruled that eighteen-year-olds could vote in national elections but not in state elections. Thus, to get eighteen-year-olds their full voting rights, the 26th Amendment.

The People's U.S. Constitution: Amendment XXVII: Limiting Congressional Pay Increases. Ratified 5/7/1992.

No law, varying the compensation for the services of the Senators and Representatives, shall take effect, until an election of Representatives shall have intervened.

This amendment was originally supposed to be a part of the Bill of Rights, submitted by James Madison to prevent Congress from voting themselves a pay raise before voters could put them out of office. The amendment was approved as one of the twelve amendments submitted to the states in September 1789, but it was not ratified along with the other ten that became the Bill of Rights as we know it today. And since there was no time limit for ratification for the amendment, it was still on the books to be ratified in the 1980s when several states did just that. Finally, in 1992 it became the last amendment to this point in time. But it was a record breaker, on the books as the longest ratification in U.S. history.

135

A Constitutional Responsibility.

OK, that's it. Take all those seven articles and twenty-seven amendments in and internalize them for your personal wealth and the betterment of all mankind. For what is more important than knowing some of the basics about your Constitutional rights as a free-living American?

If you'd really like to get on the wagon to support the spreading of the good Constitutional word, here's an opportunity. I've ordered over 100 copies of the Declaration of Independence and U.S. Constitution through The Heritage Foundation for distribution to students, family, and friends. Here's the response to my order to help with the details.

Dear Jeff Brown ,

Thank you for placing an order to receive our free pocket Constitution . This email confirms the receipt of your order.

We have received an overwhelming number of requests for the pocket Constitution --and to date have sent out over 1 million copies to people in the United States and worldwide! Because of this enthusiastic response we ask that you please allow 6 8 weeks for delivery.

You can help us continue to distribute these foundational documents to schools, Boy Scout troops, churches, veterans, civic groups, and other listeners by becoming a member of The Heritage Foundation at www.MyHeritage.org/support. We welcome and deeply appreciate your support!

So that's it. I hope this was of great help to you in understanding the Law of the Land better. Sure, there's a lot here, and it won't all come in one sitting, for sure. But if we can get more and more Americans educated as to its contents, along with other critical information (economics, critical thinking, the fallibilities of the human condition and its inherent brain failures or limitation in the extreme, ethics, morality, and so forth), we will hopefully move more toward decisions made in well-thought out fact and research along with stable, comprehensive thinking. Here's to your success and ALL of America's.

Milton Keynes UK
Ingram Content Group UK Ltd.
UKHW010204030124
435363UK00002B/387